Robert J. Bonk, PhD

Pharmacoeconomics in Perspective
A Primer on Research, Techniques, and Information

Pre-publication
REVIEWS,
COMMENTARIES,
EVALUATIONS . . .

"**I**mpressively, Dr. Bonk has ably created a comprehensive yet approachable, readable, and very understandable text on this important subject. While the book identifies pharmacoeconomics as its focus, it would also ably serve as an excellent health economics primer. Those wanting (or needing) to better understand health care decision making must read this book—and keep it nearby for future reference! The book effectively addresses all important pharmaco- economic topic areas: its rationale, types of analysis, research tech- niques, and ways of critiquing phar- macoeconomic studies."

Bart J. Harvey, MD, PhD
Assistant Professor and Director,
Community Medicine Residency
Program,
Department of Public Health Sciences,
University of Toronto,
Toronto, Canada

"*P harmacoeconomics in Perspective* is a concise introduction to this field. For most of us not trained in the field, economics (and especially a subject with a name as long as 'pharmacoeconomics') seems rather like an arcane art. Indeed, up to now, pharmacoeconomics is not a subject I have gone out of my way to learn much about. At the same time, it is difficult to ignore the influence of economics on health care. This impact is felt by everyone, from the administrators of health care plans, to physicians, to patients.

My experience indicates that most of those who must make decisions about health care are trained in medical subjects, not economic subjects. Where are these people to find information on the difference between cost-benefit analysis and cost-effective analysis? The answer is found in Dr. Bonk's book. This makes it a great resource for people who must make health care decisions based on the data and analysis provided by economists. I found Parts I (Basics of Pharmacoeconomic Research) and II (Types of Pharmacoeconomic Analyses) particularly interesting and useful. Even if you only read these two parts, you will be equipped to understand the significance and language of pharmacoeconomics. If you are involved in decisions based on this type of data, that alone is well worth the price of the book."

Terrance L. Smith, PhD
Senior Medical Editor,
Healthwise, Incorporated,
Boise, Idaho

"*P harmacoeconomics in Perspective* is a valuable collection of information on economic terminology and concepts illustrated with important published studies. Sections in the book cover outcomes research, drug development, and regulatory and ethical issues. There are useful sections on the major types of analyses, including cost of illness, cost benefit, and cost utility, but also important sections on sensitivity analyses and issues in calculating costs. The book is filled with reviews of numerous studies on many diverse disease states, including depression, peptic ulcer, stroke, asthma, obesity, cancer, transplantation, and infections. Pharmaceutical economics is an evolving research area and an understanding of these concepts is critical for survival in the dynamic health care marketplace. This text is a valuable resource for students, practitioners, and researchers. It is a significant collection of information and studies and anyone interested in health care and economics should consider this book for their personal library."

William F. McGhan, PharmD, PhD
Director, Graduate Program
in Pharmacy Administration;
Professor;
Philadelphia College of Pharmacy,
University of the Sciences,
Philadelphia, PA

Pharmacoeconomics in Perspective

A Primer on Research, Techniques, and Information

PHARMACEUTICAL PRODUCTS PRESS
Pharmaceutical Sciences
Mickey C. Smith, PhD
Executive Editor

New, Recent, and Forthcoming Titles:

A Social History of the Minor Tranquilizers: The Quest for Small Comfort in the Age of Anxiety by Mickey C. Smith

Marketing Pharmaceutical Services: Patron Loyalty, Satisfaction, and Preferences edited by Harry A. Smith and Joel Coons

Nicotine Replacement: A Critical Evaluation edited by Ovide F. Pomerleau and Cynthia S. Pomerleau

Herbs of Choice: The Therapeutic Use of Phytomedicinals by Varro E. Tyler

Interpersonal Communication in Pharmaceutical Care by Helen Meldrum

Searching for Magic Bullets: Orphan Drugs, Consumer Activism, and Pharmaceutical Development by Lisa Ruby Basara and Michael Montagne

The Honest Herbal by Varro E. Tyler

Understanding the Pill: A Consumer's Guide to Oral Contraceptives by Greg Juhn

Pharmaceutical Chartbook, Second Edition edited by Abraham G. Hartzema and C. Daniel Mullins

The Handbook of Psychiatric Drug Therapy for Children and Adolescents by Karen A. Theesen

Children, Medicines, and Culture edited by Patricia J. Bush, Deanna J. Trakas, Emilio J. Sanz, Rolf L. Wirsing, Tuula Vaskilampi, and Alan Prout

Social and Behavioral Aspects of Pharmaceutical Care edited by Mickey C. Smith and Albert I. Wertheimer

Studies in Pharmaceutical Economics edited by Mickey C. Smith

Drugs of Natural Origin: Economic and Policy Aspects of Discovery, Development, and Marketing by Anthony Artuso

Pharmacy and the U.S. Health Care System, Second Edition edited by Jack E. Fincham and Albert I. Wertheimer

Medical Writing in Drug Development: A Practical Guide for Pharmaceutical Research by Robert J. Bonk

Pharmacy and the U.S. Health Care System, Second Edition edited by Jack E. Fincham and Albert I. Wertheimer

Improving the Quality of the Medication Use Process: Error Prevention and Reducing Adverse Drug Events edited by Alan Escovitz, Dev S. Pathak, and Philip J. Schneider

Access to Experimental Drugs in Terminal Illness: Ethical Issues by Udo Schuklenk

Herbal Medicinals: A Clinician's Guide by Lucinda Miller and Wallace J. Murray

Managed Care Pharmacy: Principles and Practice edited by Albert I. Wertheimer and Robert Navarro

Pharmacoeconomics in Perspective: A Primer on Research, Techniques, and Information by Robert J. Bonk

Global Competitiveness in the Pharmaceutical Industry: The Effect of National Regulatory, Economic, and Market Factors by Madhu Agrawal

Pharmacoeconomics in Perspective
A Primer on Research, Techniques, and Information

Robert J. Bonk, PhD

Pharmaceutical Products Press
An Imprint of The Haworth Press, Inc.
New York • London • Oxford

Published by

Pharmaceutical Products Press®, an imprint of The Haworth Press, Inc., 10 Alice Street, Binghamton, NY 13904-1580

Cover design by Monica L. Seifert.

Library of Congress Cataloging-in-Publication Data

Bonk, Robert J.
    Pharmacoeconomics in perspective : a primer on research, techniques, and information / Robert J. Bonk.
        p.   cm.
    Includes bibliographical references and index.
    ISBN 0-7890-0561-1 (hardcover)
    1. Drugs—Cost effectiveness. I. Title.
RS100.B66 1999
338.4'3615'1—dc21
                                          98-47909
                                            CIP

To loved ones,
who seem to leave too quickly,
yet always remain right with us,
in our hearts.

ABOUT THE AUTHOR

Robert J. Bonk, PhD, is a supplemental faculty member at the University of Delaware, Drexel University, and the University of the Sciences in Philadelphia. He has an eclectic background that reflects many facets of the field of medical writing. A noted professional in this area, he worked for nearly two decades in the pharmaceutical industry, most recently as Manager of Medical Communications for an international firm. Dr. Bonk is locally and nationally active in the American Medical Writers Association (AMWA), and he is a former recipient of the AMWA Certificate in Pharmaceutical Writing. His recent book, *Medical Writing in Drug Development* (1998, Pharmaceutical Products Press), was selected by *Doody's Magazine* as one of the best books for 1998.

CONTENTS

Foreword

As pharmacoeconomic information becomes as ubiquitous within the next several years as sustained-release medications have already become, students and practitioners of health care must develop a basic understanding of this discipline so that they can make important clinical and managerial decisions. Today's tool of pharmacoeconomics assists in making judgments and comparisons among treatment alternatives. In five years, a health care practitioner who lacks a working knowledge of pharmacoeconomics will be as isolated as one today without a personal computer.

For health care practitioners coming to grips with this field, *Pharmacoeconomics in Perspective: A Primer on Research, Techniques, and Information* fulfills a major need. The beauty of this book is its simplicity and practical approach. Too often, we find a new source more concerned with deriving mathematical equations underlying an issue than with helping in its application. This book is intended for hands-on application.

Pharmacoeconomic principles are employed throughout the full length of the drug-use process. Consider the deliberations of a drug manufacturer. Is over $US 350 million in research and development a reasonable investment for a therapeutic market of a given size? Committees at hospitals and managed care organizations select from competing products for formulary inclusion. Physicians make similar evaluations in deciding on the optimal drug for a patient. Pharmacists determine which drugs to stock in inventory, a question also faced by drug wholesalers. In a less formal or structured environment, consumers make similar calculations: "Do I need any drug? If so, should it be prescribed by the physician or obtained OTC (over-the-counter); if the latter, should I select a name brand or a generic form?"

Such decisions cannot be made by looking at the package, no matter how long one stares. They cannot be made by studying pharmacotherapy or pathophysiology. But they can be made by employing pharmacoeconomic techniques. This book is akin to the proverbial "nuclear physics for poetry majors" course. Just as one can drive a motor vehicle without a firm understanding of how fuel injectors work, one can understand pharmacoeconomic evaluations without a mastery of linear algebra.

A working knowledge of pharmacoeconomics offers some handy by-products. Not only can one employ pharmacoeconomics for professional questions, such as whether to make or license a new drug or buy or lease a new line, but this information can also assist in making good decisions in one's private or social life.

Some books are read once and soon forgotten, whereas others are used for occasional reference; but this book has dual levels of utility. First, it is a good read once through to gain a general feeling for the area; second, it should be nearby a practitioner's desk, within easy reach to check articles when reading or when designing a study. Like a dictionary to check spelling or usage, this book should be conveniently located to check a questionable methodology, or when a reader harbors any doubts about the information.

Pharmacoeconomics in Perspective: A Primer on Research, Techniques, and Information provides the means to defend against unscrupulous promotion of new drugs, unfounded conclusions in the literature, and inappropriate methods for research studies. The title is long, but the content is straightforward, logical, and understandable by any health care practitioner who needs to use pharmacoeconomic information in today's world.

Albert I. Wertheimer, PhD, MBA
Philadelphia, Pennsylvania

Preface

Contemporary society is fascinated with superlatives such as "latest," "greatest," and "quickest." And so it is with health care as well; we all want the latest, greatest, and quickest in treatments, with all of the benefits, but none of the risks.

Benefits notwithstanding, all medical treatments come with a cost. Drugs—like public television, used cars, day care facilities, or any commodity or service on which money can be spent—consume resources in their production, delivery, and use. In economic terms, cost is more than a price tag; rather, each choice precludes other spending opportunities: once we choose to spend resources on one item, we cannot spend those same resources on something else. In other words, the opportunity is gone; our choice had an *opportunity* cost.

The latest, greatest, or quickest option may not necessarily be the best choice, considering that any decision prevents alternative uses of our resources. New tools, pharmacoeconomics included, help us to decide how to make economic choices. Complicating this process, however, is the humanistic aspect of health care. Patients are people, especially when the patients are our mothers, brothers, or children. With this perspective, I offer my primer as a first step in sorting through the complex economic issues of health care.

Acknowledgments

With this, my second book, I find myself indebted to many of the same people I was indebted to with my first book, *Medical Writing in Drug Development: A Practical Guide for Pharmaceutical Research*. But a few deserve repeated acknowledgment.

I am grateful for the continuing support of colleagues with whom I am affiliated—particularly at the University of Delaware—who stir my drive to write books such as my first, as well as this, my second. Moreover, I developed the premise for this book from a workshop that was encouraged by my associates at the American Medical Writers Association (AMWA).

And, one more acknowledgment: Heyward Brock of the University of Delaware. In 1997, he gave me the opportunity to teach one of my favorite courses, Literature and Medicine. The text I used for that course* supplied the epigraphs that introduce each major section of this book. Citing the forebears of modern medicine brings perspective to our endeavors.

---

*Downie, R. S., editor. (1994). *The Healing Arts: An Oxford Illustrated Anthology*. Oxford: Oxford University Press.

PART I:
BASIC OF PHARMACOECONOMIC RESEARCH

. . . . fix your minds on this one belief, which is certain: that nothing can harm a good man either in life or after death, and his fortunes are not a matter of indifference to the gods.

Socrates, as recorded by Plato (4th-5th century B.C.)

Pharmacoeconomic research represents a complex field that is nonetheless integral to those involved in the health care arena. Part I places this field into an easily understood framework.

Chapter 1

Pharmacoeconomics
As Outcomes Research

What distinguishes pharmacoeconomics and other branches of outcomes research from the traditional areas of health care?

Science has a way of marching forward: not always straight, not always quickly, but always inevitably forward. We like to think that society, too, always develops in the best direction. History teaches us, however, that society often takes a detour, misses an on or off ramp, and occasionally pulls off to the shoulder for a rest. Moreover, that glance in our rearview mirror momentarily reflects missed opportunities. And while we zig and zag, stop and start, or simply idle, science marches forward.

This potential disparity between the progression of science and that of society would not be as critical if not for missed opportunities and loss-of-control accidents. Not that we can—or even should—fully control our existence. We must ensure, though, that members of our society do not suffer in the bargain. Specific elements of the panoply termed "science" can more directly impinge on society than can other elements, at least at certain times. Physics, for example, rested more in academic debate before Isaac Newton proposed his mechanical theories in the seventeenth century. Application of his theories, however, subsequently powered the industrial revolutions of the eighteenth and nineteenth centuries. But in the twentieth century, the paradigm shift of quantum physics posited by Albert Einstein opened a Pandora's box: new insights into time, matter, and energy, but a potential to destroy the world that we sought to control.

UNIQUE POSITION OF HEALTH CARE

Within this panoply of science, those areas related to health care hold a unique position. Health care has catapulted to the front of the scientific race with recent advances in our understanding of microbes, genes, and technology. Spectacular achievements in vaccines, surgeries, and transplants herald an Aesculapian utopia, but eugenics and cloning peal an ethical warning. Which avenues should we allow or disallow?

Moving beyond theory, though, we encounter economics. Although we consider a threshold of health care to be a basic human right, we must also acknowledge that its production consumes resources; hence, health care stands as a finite supply against a demand of infinite proportion (Fuchs, 1984). And as a resource with a limited supply, the health care pie can only be sliced so many ways. If our society has "X" units of a drug, for example, but requires "X + Y" units to meet everyone's needs, what can be done? How can allocations of health care, and therefore life, be decided?

Health care occupies a unique position: an economic good with finite supply, but a basic right with infinite demand.

OUTCOMES OF HEALTH CARE PROGRAMS

Outcomes research provides a new vantage on health care programs. From this new vantage, society can better envision a more equitable approach to the issues surrounding health care provision. But what is outcomes research, and how is the specialty of pharmacoeconomics distinguished from it?

Basically, outcomes research, unlike traditional evaluations of efficacy or safety, seeks to quantify inputs and outputs of therapeutic options in relative economic terms (Drummond et al., 1997). What does implementation of a specific program, or provision of a particular treatment, actually cost? What are the tangible outcomes of the program or treatment? Moreover, could the resources have been better spent on some other option? By providing common economic criteria on which to judge these inputs and outputs, the relative merits of options can be weighed, allowing better decisions to be made. This concept of relativity does not harken back to our vignette of Albert Einstein; rather, relativity reflects the back-to-back measurement of seemingly disparate options through the shared idiom of economics.

Pharmacoeconomics represents the specific application of outcomes research to drugs, usually the more costly category of prescription agents. Although fundamental concepts remain the same as for other economic health care issues, the peculiarities of this slice of the health care pie position it to be better understood when considered in its own right—as in this book.

Pharmacoeconomics, like outcomes research, emphasizes the relative measurement of inputs and outputs of therapeutic options.

DEVELOPMENT OF A CRITICAL PERSPECTIVE

In the next two chapters, the prescription drug segment of health care will be dissected for expenditure data and for integration of pharmacoeconomic tools into drug development. Subsequent book parts will tackle types of pharmacoeconomic analyses, techniques of pharmacoeconomic research, and evaluation of pharmacoeconomic information. Given this book's qualitative approach, emphasizing comprehension over calculation, the final chapter offers other sources for quantitatively delving into this otherwise complex field. Overall, the book aims to provide the reader with a solid base for creating, reviewing, and using information gained from pharmacoeconomics.

Chapter 2

Health Care Expenditures
and Pharmacoeconomics

Why do health care expenditures, especially prescription drugs with out-of-pocket costs, continue to attract public scrutiny?

Today's health care consumers are fundamentally different from those of even the most recent times. Earlier consumers often accepted, without question, any and all dictates of the omniscient physician. Who else but the physician had the knowledge to determine proper treatments for our illnesses? The average layperson lacked access to medical information or, when it was available, any limited information remained undecipherable.

But today, the explosion of information changes that paternalistic approach to health care (Bonk, 1998). Health care information remains available through traditional media, such as newspapers and magazines, now written in more understandable language. And new media, especially web browsers on personal computers, easily link everyone from schoolchildren to adults with current health care information in an evolution from paternalistic to participatory roles in health care decisions (Adamcik, 1997).

FOCUS ON HEALTH CARE EXPENDITURES

Armed with increased knowledge, consumers of health care first queried, next challenged, and now influence the economics of its provision. This increased focus on health care expenditures occurred at different times in various countries, depending upon particulars of their political and cultural environments. The dra-

7

matic focal shift in the United States during the 1990s serves as a bellwether.

An aging population, maturing technology, and growing demand paved the way for increased involvement of the U.S. government and its populace in health care issues. Traditionally capitalist in approach, the U.S. government had typically intervened in market issues only as necessary: public utilities, such as water and electricity; and monopolies or their semblance, such as in transportation or telecommunications. The 1960s, however, hailed greater government intervention into issues affecting health and well-being, with Medicare and Medicaid as two prime examples (Larson, 1997).

Indeed, this increased focus of the government and consumers on health care expenditures is realistic. U.S. government analyses of health care expenditures (using 1980 and 1990 data to predict through 2030) had indicated an increasing proportion of its Gross Domestic Product (GDP) consumed by health care— roughly up to 15 percent (Burner, Waldo, and McKusick, 1992). In fact, a predicted broaching of the $US 1 trillion mark for health care expenditures by the year 2000 occurred in 1996, although with the lowest growth in expenditures (4.4 percent) since 1960 (Levit et al., 1998). Since resources consumed by health care are lost to all other uses, examination of our decision-making processes requires a firm economic grounding.

With increased availability of information, consumers have increased their focus on the health care process, including expenditures.

EMPHASIS ON PRESCRIPTION DRUGS

This focus on health care expenditures includes all sectors, from physicians and other deliverers of care to the instruments, tools, and treatments used in their services. Prescription drugs captured a critical public eye. Until recently, many insurance plans in the United States—unlike more comprehensive umbrellas through nationalized or socialized plans—excluded prescription drugs from traditional coverage. Increased participation of consumers in health care decisions challenged this tradition.

Perhaps the key impetus for extending coverage to prescription drugs stemmed from their seemingly burgeoning prices. Although prescription drugs represent only a relatively small portion (up to 10 percent) of health care expenditures, their costs remain more visible to those consumers who directly make payments (Bonk, Myers, and McGhan, 1995). Consumer demand for public or private coverage of these costs shone a spotlight on the drug market. Despite indications that this research-intensive market may not optimally respond to overt regulatory controls (Bonk et al., 1996), some degree of oversight seems warranted. This fast-paced, dynamic environment, though, requires a deliberate strategy elucidated by economic principles.

Traditionally uncovered by typical insurance plans, the increasing costs of prescription drugs quickly captured U.S. public scrutiny.

TOOLS FOR EXPENDITURE DECISIONS

But how can better decisions regarding health care expenditures, particularly the visible segment of prescription drugs, be made? Information from clinical studies of new and existing drugs, government files on Medicare and Medicaid, and articles in the popular press by crusading reformers continues to mount. With this increasing mass of information, the wheat somehow needs to be separated from the chaff. Even more difficult is the task of comparing disparate categories of clinical parameters—notably efficacy and safety—against financial data, such as prices and costs.

Economic tools can provide the answer: notably, adaptation of economic tools to the prescription-drug market. These tools fall into five principal categories (see Table 2.1). *Cost-of-illness* simply quantifies resources consumed by an illness, without focusing on outcomes. *Cost-benefit* and *cost-effectiveness* instead consider outcomes: the former, in monetary terms; the latter, as clinical measurements. *Cost-utility* is actually a special case of *cost-effectiveness*, in which outcomes are measured as preferences. Finally, *cost-minimization* compares treatments for costs only, assuming essentially identical outcomes.

Part II of this book more fully explores each of these five analytical techniques. The key message at this stage, however, is that these *pharmaco*economic analyses create a common ground on which to evaluate the disparate information categories for prescription drugs: efficacy or effectiveness, safety, quality of life and other preference measurements, and cost. Before launching into these techniques, the next chapter first considers the ways in which pharmacoeconomic research can best be integrated into the complex process of drug development.

By applying economic principles, pharmacoeconomic research provides a common ground for evaluating new drugs.

TABLE 2.1. Categories of Pharmacoeconomic Techniques

Technique	Distinguishing features
Cost-of-illness	Identifies and measures the costs of the illness itself, but *not* treatment outcomes
Cost-benefit	Measures the costs of treating an illness, along with monetary equivalents for the treatment's outcomes
Cost-effectiveness	Measures the costs of treating an illness, but using *clinical* measurements for the treatment's outcomes
Cost-utility	Measures the costs of treating an illness, but using *preference* equivalents for the treatment's outcomes
Cost-minimization	Directly compares the costs of treatment options for an illness, assuming *equivalence* of their outcomes

Chapter 3

Pharmacoeconomics
Within Drug Development

Despite being a new field requiring standardization, how can pharmaco-economic research be strategically integrated into drug development?

The process of developing a new drug is not simple. Within constraints imposed by regulatory agencies, such as the U.S. Food and Drug Administration (FDA), for public protection, research-based companies must identify, synthesize, screen, test, and then market those drugs that successfully navigate a bureaucratic maze. Now we tack these new techniques of pharmacoeconomics onto the developmental chart. How, when, and where can these research tools be strategically integrated into drug development?

Before examining this key question, an overview of drug development is necessary. Time frames, phases, studies, submissions: all of these terms require definitions. Then, the proper place of pharmacoeconomic analyses can be determined. This chapter begins with such a review of the process, emphasizing aspects most relevant to the techniques of pharmacoeconomic research.

OVERVIEW OF DRUG DEVELOPMENT

Consider viewing a 3-D representation of a new molecule on a computer screen. Rotate your molecule: visualize its crags, crevices, and crests. Adjust its atomic groups and note the physical changes that result. Now decide which version holds potential as a new drug product for the illness under study.

Not a simple prospect, is it?

Now expand your view to include the laboratory that must synthesize the chosen molecule. Then add facilities for assessing the molecule's pharmacological activity, its potential toxicities, and related parameters—using nonclinical or laboratory tests, as well as eventual clinical tests in humans. Finally, factor in sales and marketing groups who must position and promote the final production for use by consumers.

Not surprisingly, this government-monitored process consumes resources, time, and money to bring any new drug to its eventual market. In fact, despite quickening of development times for drugs targeting catastrophic illnesses such as AIDS (Acquired Immune Deficiency Syndrome), estimated parameters for drug development astound: up to a decade to bring the one successful drug— out of 10,000 on the drawing board—to market, with an approximate price tag of $US 200 million (U.S. Office of Technology Assessment, 1993).

To simplify this overview, think of drug development occurring in *phases,* a term actually used in pharmaceutical circles (Bonk, 1998a). Phases proceed chronologically so that earlier information can allow intelligent decisions on whether a drug candidate should proceed further into development. Yet phases do overlap, allowing the lengthy process of drug development to quicken its pace without jeopardizing consumer health. Although certain categories (e.g., drugs for AIDS) may follow modifications to this route, the following list identifies main phases of drug development. Table 3.1 gives more detail on these phases; Figure 3.1 illustrates their time relationships.

- *Design Phase:* early work on the disease and potential designs for its drugs
- *Nonclinical Phase:* research in laboratory or animal settings, not in humans

- *Clinical Phases I, II, and III:* research in humans, under regulatory scrutiny
- *Submission Phase:* documentation of research findings for government review
- *Clinical Phase IV:* additional follow-up, especially for safety, once marketed

Overall, this progression of drug development through phases ensures that new drugs can be adequately assessed without undue jeopardy to consumers. For example, a candidate without sufficient pharmacological activity (i.e., for intended use) or with toxicities would not proceed into clinical tests. One with safety risks exceeding efficacy benefits would not be approved for marketing, or would be pulled if problems later arose.

TABLE 3.1. Phases of Drug Development

Phase	Involvement*	Objectives
Design	Molecular Modeling	Theoretically design drug candidates
	Medicinal Chemistry	Realistically synthesize new drugs
Nonclinical	Pharmacology	Test activity in animals or simulations
	Toxicology	Assess early safety for potential risks
Clinical:		
I	Clinical Pharmacology	Identify kinetics, metabolism, and dose
II	Clinical Research	Profile efficacy and safety under restrictions
III	Clinical Research	Profile efficacy and safety in wider groups
Submission	Regulatory Affairs	Negotiate approval for marketing
Clinical IV	Medical Affairs	Conduct trials for new groups or uses
	Safety Surveillance	Monitor safety during drug marketing

*Typical group names in pharmaceutical companies, not fully comprehensive.

FIGURE 3.1. Generalized Time Frames for Drug Development

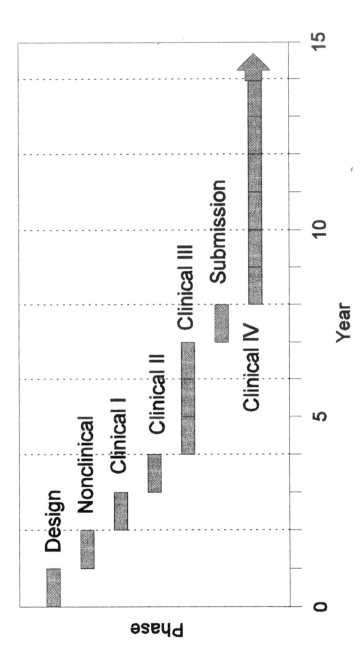

Phased development of new prescription drugs allows pharmaceutical companies to bring products to market without jeopardizing consumer health.

REGULATIONS FOR PHARMACOECONOMIC DATA

Because pharmacoeconomic research represents a twist on traditional types of drug research, regulations and requirements remain in a state of flux. The U.S. FDA, for example, does not yet mandate inclusion of pharmacoeconomic data to gain approval; however, other countries, notably Australia and Canada, do require pharmacoeconomic information within a submission package to allow marketing of a drug (Wechsler, 1991). Surely, other countries will follow suit—especially given ongoing moves toward standardization of regulatory requirements on a global basis, such as the International Committee for Harmonization (ICH) (Nightingale, 1995).

Furthermore, regulatory approval to market a drug does not seal the deal by any means. New drugs must not only be promoted to physicians and other prescribers, but also must gain approval for reimbursement by insurance groups, managed care institutions, and hospital formulary boards. These groups increasingly demand pharmacoeconomic evidence for drug prices and benefits. And promotional materials, such as in medical journals, must be grounded in scientific information (Bonk, 1998b), as could be gained from soundly conducted pharmacoeconomic research (Bonk, 1993).

Although not required by all regulatory agencies, pharmacoeconomic information is gaining in importance for the successful marketing of a new drug.

INTEGRATION OF PHARMACOECONOMIC RESEARCH

Given the currently loose standards for pharmacoeconomic requirements, how can a company strategically integrate this key research into the development process for a new drug? Before answering this question, a key distinction needs to be made between *efficacy* and *effectiveness*. Efficacy refers to the beneficial actions of a drug under controlled or restricted conditions, as occur in research studies. Effectiveness, however, reflects the beneficial actions as experienced without such restrictions, once a drug becomes used outside of a research setting. Because prices, costs, and other economic parameters reflect the real world, so to speak, pharmacoeconomic research should focus on effectiveness, rather than efficacy.

Pharmacoeconomic studies, therefore, have generally been included within Clinical Phase IV as postmarketing or epidemiological analyses (Arikian et al., 1992). Although Phase IV studies still occur under regulations, some relaxation allows greater generalizability of results to the real world. Epidemiological or surveillance studies do, in fact, collect data from real-world use. But such trials can be vulnerable to vagary, given their lack of the ideal clinical study's scientific rigor.

Pressures to expedite development, however, continue to translate into adapting pharmacoeconomic studies to earlier phases (Bootman, Townsend, and McGhan, 1996). One manner in which to accomplish this goal, without jeopardizing the data's usefulness, would be to collect pharmacoeconomic measurements within Clinical Phase III. At this research stage, fewer restrictions than in Clinical Phases I and II would at least increase the generalizability of the results. Earlier information nonetheless permits companies to focus research funds on those drug candidates with the greatest potential for success (Wyse, Peel, and Kirby, 1997). Pharmacoeconomic techniques that simply amass data on the illness itself, such as in cost-minimization, could be conducted anywhere along the development path; updates to such analyses, though, would most likely be needed if the health care environment maintains its current volatility.

Of course, recognizing that trials conducted earlier in development would have rigorous scientific restrictions would be essential in their interpretation. These types of issues are addressed in Part III, after detailing specific techniques in Part II.

Earlier integration of pharmacoeconomic research must account for the expected decrease in generalizability of results.

Evaluation I

Pharmacoeconomic Research

Have you understood the key messages of Part I? To check, answer these questions. Then compare your answers with those at the end of this section. For follow-up study, review the relevant chapters noted in these answers.

QUESTIONS

1. Health care is often considered a basic human right that should be guaranteed to all. Why, then, should economic tools be applied to health care decisions?

2. Why can pharmacoeconomics be considered as a subset or specialization of outcomes research?

3. How has greater access to information spurred the current focus, in both public and private sectors, on health care expenditures?

4. Given that prescription drugs actually comprise a relatively small portion of total health care expenditures, why does this category capture special attention?

5. How do pharmacoeconomic techniques aid in evaluations of prescription drugs, which involve a range of parameters, from efficacy and safety to quality of life?

6. Why does drug development, a time-consuming and re-source-intensive process, proceed through discrete phases?

7. Since not all countries require pharmacoeconomic information for licensure of a new drug, why should companies bother to conduct such research?

8. How do the related concepts of efficacy and effectiveness link to the timing of pharmacoeconomic studies in the development of a new drug?

ANSWERS

1. Although understandably viewed as a basic human right, health care also must be allocated. Therefore, health care occupies a unique position as an economic good with a finite supply, despite a seemingly infinite demand. Techniques of pharmacoeconomics can help in the difficult decisions of health care allocation. *(Chapter 1)*

2. Outcomes research comprises techniques that measure the inputs and outputs of therapeutic options. With such techniques, the economic nature of health care allocation can be better understood. Because the prescription-drug market has peculiarities, relative to other health care segments, pharmacoeconomics tailors basic outcomes tools to this important expenditure category. *(Chapter 1)*

3. Greater access to information, such as through the popular press and especially the Internet, fosters increased participation of individuals in their health care, as well as in expenditures on that care. Moreover, this knowledge coincides with a movement toward greater participation in health care decisions. *(Chapter 2)*

4. In countries without socialized medicine, prescription drugs sometimes remain uncovered by private insurance plans. Hence, consumers directly experience these costs, fostering greater scrutiny of this segment. *(Chapter 2)*

5. With their economic basis, pharmacoeconomic techniques provide a common ground for comparing seemingly disparate categories of drug characteristics. Moreover, pharmacoeconomic research includes the important category of cost, a crucial element in decisions of health care allocation. *(Chapter 2)*

6. The phased approach to drug development allows companies to whittle down a large number of potential drugs to ever smaller numbers of likely candidates that proceed to the next phase in development. In this way, consumer health can be safeguarded, while expediting the development of new drugs. *(Chapter 3)*

7. Although not all countries legislatively mandate inclusion of pharmacoeconomic information in regulatory submissions, increasing international standardization portends this inevitability. Moreover, successful marketing of a drug depends on pharmacoeconomic information to gain acceptance by a plethora of institutions, as well as to underpin promotional materials. *(Chapter 3)*

8. Efficacy, which measures a drug's actions under controlled conditions, lacks the generalizability of effectiveness, which is only gained from widespread use of a new drug. Earlier integration of pharmacoeconomic research into development requires a balance between scientific rigor and generalizability. *(Chapter 3)*

PART II:
TYPES OF PHARMACOECONOMIC
ANALYSES

The cases do not fall under any art or precept.
Instead the agents themselves must all the time consider
what is appropriate to the particular occasion,
just as in medicine or navigation.

Aristotle (4th century B.C.)

In Part II, each of the five principal types of pharmacoeconomic analyses are defined. Examples of appropriate applications illustrate key similarities and differences.

Chapter 4

Cost-of-Illness Analysis

What distinguishes cost-of-illness analysis from other types of pharmaco-economic analyses?

Before launching into full-scale pharmacoeconomic analyses of new or existing drugs, researchers require baseline information on the cost of the illness to be treated. Baseline information on the cost that an illness imposes on society mirrors the baseline information typically collected for other descriptive parameters of the disease:

- *prevalence*, the number of existing cases in a population
- *incidence*, the number of new cases in a given time period
- *morbidity*, the frequency of an illness's effects on individuals
- *mortality*, the rate at which an illness prematurely causes death

BASELINE MEASURES OF COST

Similar to these other baseline measurements, the cost of a disease can provide useful information for determining how to develop new drug treatments. Cost-of-illness analysis simply represents a tool for quantifying the costs to society of a disease, without considering any of its treatments. In effect, cost-of-illness analysis provides a common framework through which to assess the potential for developing a drug to treat a particular disease.

For example, consider a pharmaceutical company seeking to expand its areas of research and development. Should it venture into treatments for depression or related mental illnesses? Several questions internal to the company must first be considered, such as whether the company has staff experienced in this disease area. Outside the company, are existing treatments for this disease sufficiently sparse for a new drug to enter the marketing arena? Moreover, does society need another treatment?

Along with these key questions must be posed a basic business issue: Does this disease area have a robust market with enough potential for the company to recoup its investment into developing a new drug for its treatment? As described in Part I of this book, drug development—especially for a new disease area—requires a long-term investment of significant amounts of resource, including both money and personnel. By measuring the financial toll that a disease exacts on society (Luce and Elixhauser, 1996), cost-of-illness analysis can help answer this question.

By measuring a disease's baseline costs to society, cost-of-illness analysis allows sound decisions on research investments.

COST-OF-ILLNESS EXAMPLES

Perhaps the best way to understand cost-of-illness analysis is to examine some examples of published literature on such research. This section reviews examples that illustrate the general principles of cost-of-illness research; readers are encouraged to explore additional examples on their own.

Peptic Ulcer

A 1989 survey on digestive diseases found that recently occurring ulcers were associated with annual expenditures of $US

5.65 billion. Because 40 percent of patients with ulcers had visited a physician at least five times during the twelve months before the study, opportunities exist for overall cost savings from better treatment of ulcers (Sonnenberg and Everhart, 1997).

Stroke

The incidence of stroke is high: approximately 500,000 occurrences a year in the United States alone. The costs associated with stroke can be segregated into two main categories (as discussed in Chapter 11): direct costs from caring for the patient, and indirect costs from earnings or revenue lost to society from incapacitation of the patient. For stroke in the United States, these costs total $US 30 billion, with slightly less than half ($US 13 billion) attributable to indirect costs (Taylor, 1997). This cost-of-illness analysis of stroke, a major illness in developed countries such as the United States, indeed highlights the importance of considering all relevant costs of the disease. If we fail to do so, we run the risk of underestimating a disease's economic burden on society.

Asthma

Similar to stroke, asthma represents an illness with high expenditures. In the United States, total costs in 1987 reached $US 5.8 billion; unlike the breakdown for stroke, however, direct costs of asthma predominate at about 88 percent (Smith et al., 1997). Interestingly, this cost-of-illness analysis identified a high-cost group of patients who comprised only 20 percent of those with asthma, but who in fact consumed more than 80 percent of all resource expenditures. Thus, treatments that target this high-cost group may offer the greatest opportunity for lowering asthma's economic burden on society.

Obesity

A cost-of-illness analysis of obesity in New Zealand illustrates the importance of clearly identifying assumptions for economic calculations (see Chapter 12). Costs in 1991 were aggregated for major illnesses associated with obesity, including non-insulin dependent diabetes, coronary heart disease, hypertension, gallstones, colon cancer, and postmenopausal breast cancer. Estimated costs attributable to obesity totaled $NZ 135 million, a conservative estimate because only six of all related illnesses were included in these calculations (Swinburn et al., 1997). Furthermore, the cost-of-illness analysis indicates the need for careful comparisons across countries; for example, this somewhat low expenditure, when converted to a percentage (2.5 percent) of total health care costs, is equivalent to that spent on obesity in other countries.

Scleroderma

In contrast to the previous diseases, scleroderma is rather rare, affecting fewer than 100,000 people in the United States. Cost estimations for rare diseases typically suffer from a lack of reliable data. Although its annual costs reach only $US 1.5 billion, scleroderma equates to a cost of $US 300,000 per death because of the earnings lost during the long-term course of this illness (Wilson, 1997). Hence, researchers must be careful not to dismiss diseases with low aggregate cost to society, but with serious impact on the afflicted individuals.

Cost-of-illness analysis provides basic data for societal decisions, but the impact on the individual must not be forgotten.

Chapter 5

Cost-Benefit Analysis

What distinguishes cost-benefit analysis from other types of pharmaco-economic analyses?

Unlike cost-of-illness analysis (as discussed in Chapter 4), cost-benefit analysis assesses both the inputs, or costs, of a disease along with the outputs, or benefits, of a treatment or treatments. Costs in this regard reflect expenditures on the disease and the treatment; benefits quantify the outcomes of the treatment—indeed, "benefits" may be positive, neutral, or negative, depending on the outcome achieved. A treatment that works would have positive benefits, whereas one that did not work as had been intended would lack benefits, or perhaps be detrimental altogether.

In this chapter, the differentiating characteristics of a cost-benefit analysis are examined, along with situations in which this type of pharmacoeconomic analysis might be applied. Examples from the literature illustrate these uses.

COMMON DENOMINATOR FOR COMPARISON

Cost-benefit analysis distinguishes itself from other types of pharmacoeconomic analysis by its quantification of inputs and outputs in one common language: money. Through this common denominator, the costs and benefits can be directly compared for a treatment or other therapeutic intervention; a net outcome or yield, in financial terms, allows the intervention's overall value to be assessed (McGhan, 1996). With this analysis, a researcher can determine if a treatment's outcomes might exceed requisite financial investment for its implementation.

Consider, for example, a government agency deciding whether free influenza vaccination should be provided to its represented society. Total costs of implementing such an intervention can be determined (see Chapter 11), and then compared with the expected financial benefits of not having to treat as many cases of influenza. (Chapter 9 details other types of benefits to be considered for a societal perspective.) Will expected benefits exceed known costs for influenza vaccination? A cost-benefit analysis provides data on which the agency's decision can be grounded.

Because cost-benefit analysis reduces all terms to the common denominator of money, in theory this approach has broader applications than other pharmacoeconomic analyses do (Drummond et al., 1997). This theoretical advantage, however, can lose its edge in practical application. In the example of influenza vaccination, the benefits to society of lessening the incidence and severity of influenza may not be straightforward to calculate: palliative treatments can be priced, as can doctor or clinic visits, but what about lost productivity to the individual who remains home from work for several days? How will benefits be measured in monetary terms for different levels of risk to influenza among children, adults, and seniors? Thus, cost-benefit analysis has broader uses, provided that monetary conversions of all appropriate benefits can be obtained.

Cost-benefit analysis reduces the inputs and outputs of an intervention to comparable monetary terms.

APPLICATIONS OF COST-BENEFIT ANALYSIS

Given their potentially wide applications, cost-benefit analyses can be used in a variety of ways. First, cost-benefit analysis can assess the net monetary outcome of a single intervention, rather than only as a comparison against another intervention. This net yield can be measured as benefits minus costs, or as a ratio of costs to benefits. In either case, a tangible value results for the particular intervention. Other analysis types typically measure the yield of an intervention relative to an alternative one (as discussed in the subsequent chapters of Part II). Thus, cost-benefit analysis allows quantification of an absolute, rather than a relative, value.

Second, cost-benefit analysis can be used like other pharmacoeconomic analyses in comparing the net yields of more than one intervention for a disease. For example, the net outcomes of controlling diabetes or hypertension first through diet and exercise, rather than immediately through medication, could be quantified and then compared. Hence, cost-benefit analysis allows comparison, in monetary terms, of alternatives for treating a particular disease.

Third, and unlike other pharmacoeconomic analyses, cost-benefit analysis allows the direct quantitative comparison of interventions for *different* diseases. At first, such comparisons might appear unnecessary, and indeed these issues do not usually arise in the clinical setting of treating a single patient. But think more widely to a government agency, hospital board, insurance group, or other administrative body. Working within set budgets, these groups must often decide on the allocation of funds among disparate alternatives. Should a hospital implement an education program to raise the public's awareness of lead poisoning from old paint, or channel those funds instead to purchase a new diagnostic instrument?

Through its common monetary denominator, cost-benefit analysis provides the financial data on which such a decision's debate can at least begin. Obviously, other factors beyond straight financial yield must be considered in these crucial decisions for any group with a limited budget. The purpose of economics overall is to provide tools and criteria through which decisions on allocation of any limited resource—which includes health care—can be made (Feldstein, 1993). Cost-benefit analysis can provide the tools, but we in society must set and interpret the criteria for making decisions.

With its potentially wider applications, cost-benefit analysis can be used to assess single or multiple interventions.

COST-BENEFIT EXAMPLES

Perhaps the best way to understand cost-benefit analysis is to examine some examples of published literature on such research. This section reviews examples that illustrate the general principles of cost-benefit research; readers are encouraged to explore additional examples on their own.

Influenza Vaccination

As noted earlier in this chapter, economic evaluations of wide implementation often lend themselves to cost-benefit analysis. Such an evaluation of vaccination for influenza among the elderly in New Zealand quantified in monetary terms this plan's benefits and costs, and their difference or net benefit (Scott and Scott, 1996). Several iterations of this analysis allowed the net benefits of influenza vaccination of the elderly to be considered from a number of different perspectives (as discussed in Chapter 9).

Birth Weight

As implied with the previous situation of the elderly, cost-benefit analysis can be applied to any age group. Treatment of infants categorized as low birth weight must be tailored to their special needs; however, at what point do the costs of such treatments exceed their benefits? Treatment with recombinant human erythropoietin (r-HuEPO), for example, was determined to be cost-beneficial in infants weighing less than 750 g at birth, but not for those weighing up to 1500 g (Asch and Wedgwood, 1997). Selective use of r-HuEPO may therefore provide better management of costs and treatments.

Poison-Related Hospitalizations

For another age group, namely children, high expenditures result from ingestion of poisons. Can these costs be lowered? A cost-benefit analysis of poison-related hospitalizations used charge data, along with length of stay (LOS) in the hospital, over four years to answer this question (Woolf, Wieler, and Greenes, 1997). Despite increased cases over this period, charges and LOS significantly decreased, and at a greater rate than for a comparison group of other pediatric hospitalizations. Further analysis identified three agents—acetaminophen, lead, and antidepressant drugs—as the most common and the most costly ones for poison-related hospitalizations. Thus, interventions targeting these three agents should provide the best return on investment.

Case Management

Costs and benefits of an illness can include more than typical *direct* costs of treatments, such as drugs, physician fees, and hospitalization. *Indirect* costs, such as wages lost during an illness, can also represent major expenditures and may need to be considered as *marginal* costs accruing for each additional effective treatment (as discussed in Chapter 11). Lost productivity formed a key category of expenditures in a Swedish study of patients absent from work for long periods because of minor chronic disease (Timpka et al., 1997). A team-based rehabilitation model for case management proved to be cost-beneficial to society on a marginal basis with indirect costs.

Ulcer Modeling

In addition to inherent complexity, cost-benefit calculations may also require longer-term data than yet available. Duodenal ulcer, for example, can now be treated by eradicating the bacterium *Helicobacter pylori*, potentially causative in many cases. Because this treatment is relatively new, a Belgian group compared short-term results with long-term predictions from Markov-chain simulations (Deltenre and Ilunga, 1997). This model predicted greater savings by eradicating this bacterium than by treatment of gastric episodes with anti-secretory drugs. However, such models depend on specific assumptions underlying calculations (as discussed in Chapter 12), thereby constraining the robustness of the results.

Complex cost-benefit calculations may depend on model assumptions that require further substantiation.

Chapter 6

Cost-Effectiveness Analysis

What distinguishes cost-effectiveness analysis from other types of pharmacoeconomic analyses?

Cost-effectiveness analysis builds on the common denominator of money in cost-benefit analysis (as discussed in Chapter 5). In fact, these two analysis types represent the most commonly encountered pharmacoeconomic applications, as each allows direct comparison of alternative treatments for a particular disease. But unlike cost-benefit analysis, cost-effectiveness analysis avoids the complications of reducing all outcomes to a monetary basis. Instead, cost-effectiveness analysis retains the main therapeutic outcome—such as a reduction of blood pressure or the years of life saved—as the measure of effectiveness.

In this chapter, this differentiating characteristic of cost-effectiveness analysis is explored for theoretical considerations and typical applications. Literature examples solidify understanding of this key pharmacoeconomic tool.

THERAPEUTIC MEASURES OF EFFECTIVENESS

Cost-effectiveness analysis relies on proper selection of a therapeutic measure or outcome to capture the essence of the intervention's usefulness. Does the therapy increase hemoglobin levels in patients with anemia? Or allow post-surgical patients to heal more quickly? Or perhaps even decrease mortality for patients with cancer? Two or more therapeutic interventions, often drugs, can be compared directly for their costs to achieve the selected outcome. For example, what are the respective costs of aspirin and streptokinase for reducing mortality in patients after a myocardial infarction?

Because the alternative therapies may have different costs as well as different levels of effectiveness, this pharmacoeconomic approach often uses a ratio of outcome achieved to cost expended. Calculation of this cost, however, depends on the research perspective (as discussed in Chapter 9), along with inclusion of appropriate categories of cost (as discussed in Chapter 11). Regardless of these complications, use of ratios of cost-effectiveness allows alternative therapies to be compared more meaningfully on a relative scale (Chrischilles, 1996). By comparing these ratios, a researcher can then select a particular therapy for the situation at hand.

Determining effectiveness measures, however, introduces its own complications. Does the situation lend itself to a single, clear yardstick for effectiveness? Reduction in pain scores, for example, would seem logical for comparing two analgesic drugs. But for comparing therapies for anxiety, should patient satisfaction be assessed along with a more objective measurement of mental state? Careful examination of the therapeutic situation thus should precede definitive selection of the effectiveness measure, so that secondary measures may be considered as adjuncts to the principal cost-effectiveness analysis (Drummond et al., 1997).

Cost-effectiveness analysis relies on careful selection of outcome measures for meaningful comparison of alternative therapies.

APPLICATIONS OF COST-EFFECTIVENESS ANALYSIS

Perhaps the most universal of pharmacoeconomic analyses, cost-effectiveness analysis relatively positions the alternative therapies for the same disease or indication. Because therapeutic decisions typically involve selection of an appropriate therapy for a patient or group of patients, these two applications require further exploration.

First, how can cost-effectiveness analysis be applied to therapeutic decisions on a patient-by-patient basis? This tool does not purport to supersede careful, individual attention by the patient's health care provider. Rather, results from such analyses add to the provider's repository of information. Understanding the relative merits—both cost and effectiveness—of alternative therapies for the patient's own situation allows a health care provider to recommend a treatment more acceptable to the patient. Indeed, as individual patients increasingly participate in decisions regarding their own health care (Adamcik, 1997), the information gleaned from cost-effectiveness research potentially fosters greater rapport between patient and provider. For example, a patient without insurance coverage for prescription drugs might wish to know trade-offs, if any, between cost and effectiveness for two different therapies for a chronic condition, such as asthma.

Second, can this application on a patient-by-patient basis be extended to groups of patients? This broader application of cost-effectiveness analysis represents perhaps its more likely scenario. Insurance groups, formulary boards, and hospital pharmacies, among other groups, must determine which of all available treatments to include in their respective armamentaria. Although five diuretic agents for hypertension may be therapeutically redundant, for instance, five antibiotics for nosocomial pneumonia may actually be recommended for one institution because of emergent microbial resistance. Decisions on specific therapies, the number of alternatives, and appropriate treatment protocols can thus benefit from quantitative data on their cost and effectiveness, as well as their advantages and disadvantages (Freeman, 1996).

Applicable to decisions on both the individual and group levels, cost-effectiveness research thus represents a particularly robust form of pharmacoeconomic analysis. But such decisions themselves remain difficult: any therapeutic option brings its requisite disadvantages, whether in terms of cost or outcome. Hence, decision makers must be attuned to the nuances affecting all types of pharmacoeconomic research.

Cost-effectiveness analysis provides one level of information on which to base treatment decisions for individuals and groups.

COST-EFFECTIVENESS EXAMPLES

Perhaps the best way to understand cost-effectiveness analysis is to examine some examples of published literature on such research. This section reviews examples that illustrate the general principles of cost-effectiveness research; readers are encouraged to explore additional examples on their own.

ACE Inhibitors in Post-Myocardial Infarction

Comparison of the relative cost-effectiveness of alternative therapies represents this research tool's primary application, as exemplified by a study of angiotensin-converting enzyme (ACE) inhibitors after myocardial infarction (McMurray et al., 1997). Ratios of cost for each year of life gained varied with drug cost, indicating strategies for maximizing the use of ACE inhibitors in this high-risk group.

Dosages of Lovastatin for Hyperlipidemia

As a variation on the theme of comparing different drugs for the same indication, cost-effectiveness research can also compare different dosage levels of the same drug. Estimating the costs for each year of life saved in reducing cholesterol allowed comparison of different levels of lovastatin to treat hyperlipidemia in preventing coronary disease (Perreault et al., 1998). A cost of $US 50,000 was defined as "acceptable" for each year of life. On this basis, a low dosage (20 mg/day) proved to be acceptable for men and women of middle age and with cholesterol levels of at least 6.67 mmol/L, whereas a high dosage (80 mg/day) could not be justified as a primary preventative measure.

Adjuvant Therapy for Colon Cancer

Applying cost-effectiveness information to therapeutic decisions for individual patients formed the focus of a review of available adjuvant therapies for colon cancer (Macdonald, 1997). In advanced (Stage III) cases of this disease, adjuvant therapies generally appear cost-effective, in some cases below $US 5,000 for each year of life saved. Thus, choices for an individual patient may emphasize not cost, but rather the specific nuances of the situation. For example, some treatments achieving the same level of effectiveness when given for shorter periods at higher doses might additionally introduce a greater likelihood of untoward side effects.

Decision-Support Systems for Angioplasty

As reflected in some previous examples, new treatments may have higher costs that preclude their routine use in patient groups with lower risk. A computer model was designed to determine cost-effectiveness levels of newer agents for patients at low risk for coronary artery disease (Eisenstein et al., 1997). Calculation of "break-even" points at which these therapies reached cost-neutrality identified the highest allowable costs for cost-effectiveness to be realized. Such research supports not only policy groups devising health care strategies, but also pharmaceutical firms funding the research and development of new therapeutic agents.

Diagnosis of Tuberculosis in Kenya

Cost-effectiveness analysis can also apply to difficult decisions of limited funding for therapeutic interventions in developing countries. Kenya served as the geographic locus for a comparison of two diagnostic techniques for tuberculosis: polymerase chain reaction and direct smear microscopy (Roos et al., 1998). In this case, the outcome of effectiveness was the correct diagnosis of a patient with tuberculosis—an interesting twist of effectiveness for a policy-level decision. Moreover, polymerase chain reaction was expected to be more specific and sensitive for this measurement, but at a known greater cost. Given this trade-off, direct smear microscopy proved to be almost twice as cost-effective, allowing for better allocation of Kenya's limited funds.

Decisions based on cost-effectiveness research can vary in interpretation, depending upon the setting in which they are applied.

Chapter 7

Cost-Utility Analysis

What distinguishes cost-utility analysis from other types of pharmaco-economic analyses?

With its versatility for application within a variety of settings, cost-effectiveness analysis (see Chapter 6) fragments into special cases. One of these specializations of cost-effectiveness analysis is cost-utility analysis, in which efficacy focuses on *utility* for the individual patient. In other words, how does a patient view the treatment? Perhaps a treatment appears attractive to the patient's health care provider for cost-benefit or cost-effectiveness ratios. But did those ratios adequately reflect more subtly subjective measures, such as tremors that limit the patient's painting or sewing hobby, undue sleepiness that renders driving precarious at best, or an inhibited sexual function that stresses a relationship?

This chapter delineates the differentiating characteristics of cost-utility analysis, with literature examples demonstrating application of this pharmacoeconomic specialty.

MEASUREMENTS OF UTILITY

As a seemingly esoteric parameter, utility often eludes simple, direct quantitative measurement. How can we quantify the value that an individual places on an aspect of health and well-being? Philosophers—from Jeremy Bentham of the utilitarian school, to Immanuel Kant and his opposing categorical imperative—debated this issue in the past; the debate flourishes today, albeit along more specific lines, such as health.

For the purpose of pharmacoeconomic analyses, however, utility can be used in its strict economic sense: the level or degree of satisfaction and well-being. Cost-utility analysis thus measures the cost for a therapy to achieve a given change in a patient's health status; as a ratio, this balance can be expressed as the cost per unit of utility (Coons and Kaplan, 1996). Typically, cost-utility analysis expresses health outcomes in terms of the QALY, or the quality-adjusted life year (Drummond et al., 1997). More specifically, the degree of health utility obtained with the therapy tempers the length of life extension. For example, an extra year of life with constant pain from a treatment might be only half as valuable to a patient as would a year of perfect health, thereby equating to 0.5 (not 1.0) QALY.

But how useful is the QALY itself? As a theoretical construct, the QALY may be of limited applicative value in empirical research (Pathak, 1996). Thus, the QALY measures may themselves be useful only when viewed in a wider social context across the entire range of health care (Nord, 1994). But in a semiquantitative sense, patients may indicate a ranking of possible outcomes so that relative utilities can be quantified. As with any other economic commodity, health care must be bartered for against other products that a patient could buy with his or her finite resources. In this sense of a "trade-off," would the patient opt for two extra years of a painful existence or half a year in a disease-free state? Cost-utility analysis, then, seeks to measure this difficult decision process.

Shortcomings notwithstanding, utility measurements are increasingly applied in pharmacoeconomic analyses because many diseases require inclusion of the patient's predilections or preferences for particular outcomes. Often, these preferences can be assessed through measurement of the patient's "quality of life," for which a variety of measuring instruments are available: from global scores for generic tests irrespective of disease, to specific tests tailored for factors specific to syndromes (Souetre, Qing, and Hardens, 1994). Cancer, for example, represents a disease for which quality of life greatly affects selection of therapeutic options. In fact, utility may be used not just in cost-utility analyses of drugs or treatments, but also in assisting the practitioner and patient in choosing an optimal treatment (Cassileth, 1992).

Because cost-utility analyses opens a Pandora's box of questions, how might its applicability to specific situations be determined? Factors to be considered include relevance of utility or quality of life to the disease state, as well as the need for a comprehensive measure of outcome that includes both mortality and morbidity (Drummond et al., 1997). These situations form the crux of the next section, which provides examples of cost-utility analysis.

Despite inherent difficulties with measuring a preference or utility, cost-utility analysis contributes to difficult treatment decisions.

COST-UTILITY EXAMPLES

Perhaps the best way to understand cost-utility analysis is to examine examples of published literature on such research. This section reviews examples that illustrate the situations in which cost-utility research can be applied; readers are encouraged to explore additional examples on their own.

Treatments for Breast Cancer

As stated earlier in this chapter, cancer represents the type of disease state for which cost-utility research can be useful. Women with anthracycline-resistant breast cancer, for example, typically survive only up to about nine months; hence, a therapy that can improve the quality of remaining life can be crucially optimal. Two treatments for this severe form of breast cancer, namely docetaxel and paclitaxel, were compared, using a QALY calculated from the patient's preference for health states and treatment outcomes (Yee, 1997). A slight advantage for docetaxel over paclitaxel, although only about 0.09 QALY per patient, translated into 33 days of perfect health—meaningful for patients with only nine months to live.

Threshold for Lung Transplantation

With so many competing demands on resources, society faces difficult decisions regarding the allocation of funds for specific types of health care. Lung transplantation, for example, can save an individual's life. But at how high of a cost? A retrospective study on lung recipients at one institution over six months sought to generate some preliminary data on the threshold return-on-investment of this expensive surgery. On the basis of quality of well-being, the median utility score was 0.599; with a median cost of $US 94,324 for each surgery, a gain in survival of 2.7 years per patient would be the threshold for this treatment to be cost-justifiable to society (Gartner et al., 1997).

Programs for HIV Prevention

Should society allocate finite funds for organ transplantation or for preventing wider spread of existing diseases, as caused by HIV (human immunodeficiency virus)? Such societal decisions depend on techniques such as cost-utility analysis that place these disparate situations on a common playing field. Periodic recalculation may also be needed when treatments and costs both increase, as for HIV. A recalculation using a lifetime medical cost of $US 195,000 to avert a QALY loss of 11.23 for each infected patient found a cost-utility ratio favoring HIV prevention among alternative programs seeking societal funding (Holtgrave and Pinkerton, 1997). Hence, cost-utility analysis can be similar to cost-benefit analysis (see Chapter 5) in applicability across disparate types of treatment or funding scenarios.

Prevention of Opportunistic Retinitis

Patients with late-stage HIV infection have a poor prognosis. Hence, morbidity must join mortality within treatment strategies, particularly for preventing opportunistic infections that can devastate the patient's remaining life. The incidence of one such opportunistic infection, cytomegalovirus (CMV) retinitis, can be reduced by prophylactic use of oral ganciclovir. This costly treatment is not well tolerated by patients, however, indicating that a careful comparison of various outcome parameters must be conducted. One decision analysis used these parameters in a cost-utility analysis of ganciclovir versus no prophylaxis in preventing retinitis in this patient group (Moore and Chaisson, 1997). This analysis found that prophylactic ganciclovir may not be justifiable unless a greater response rate for efficacy can be achieved (Moore and Chaisson, 1997).

Radiation for Malignant Glioma

Because of its outcome component, cost-utility analysis hinges on astute choice of measurement parameters. Comparison of calculated ratios with actual results can add considerably to refinement of these evolving techniques. In one such evaluation (Konski et al., 1997), calculated cost-utility values were compared with published results for quality-adjusted survival in patients receiving radiation therapy for malignant glioma. Among tested options, the treatment with the lowest cost per QALY also produced the longest quality-adjusted survival. Inclusion of cost and utility parameters in trials such as this one continue to enhance this pharmacoeconomic tool.

Cost-utility analysis will only improve through application in health care research.

Chapter 8

Cost-Minimization Analysis

What distinguishes cost-minimization analysis from other types of pharmacoeconomic analyses?

Along with cost-utility analysis (as described in Chapter 7), a second specialty case of cost-effectiveness analysis (see Chapter 6) exists: cost-minimization analysis. Its title alone entices interest, as *minimizing cost* remains a key consideration in most—if not all—pharmacoeconomic analyses. In this case, though, minimization of cost refers not to techniques for driving down expenditures explicitly, but rather to a comparison of costs for alternative interventions with equivalent outcomes (Bootman, Townsend, and McGhan, 1996).

Incorrect supposition of outcome equivalency, however, could indeed undermine the validity of an otherwise sound pharmacoeconomic study. This chapter thus defines the conditions under which cost-minimization analysis should be used, as well as when this speciality technique may require modification.

EQUIVALENCY OF OUTCOMES

Consider a medical situation not uncommon in practice: two antibiotics, one the newest in an established class, the other a generic form of an older drug in that same class, and that could each be appropriately prescribed for a patient's infection. Both have been scientifically shown to eradicate the identified bacterium in the same number of days, with the same rates of success, and with essentially identical chances of a limited number of side effects. Which antibiotic should be prescribed?

Under the parameters of this hypothetical scenario, the simplest approach would be to determine which of these two antibiotics costs less. Presumably, the generic form of the older drug of the same class would be chosen.

When extrapolated from this one hypothetical case to a pharmacoeconomic analysis, parameters become more complex. How commonly might two different treatments have identical (or roughly so) patterns of outcomes? Equivalency assumes that the appropriate measures of efficacy and safety were used (as explained in Chapter 10). If this assumption of outcome equivalency is true, then the analysis essentially reduces cost-minimization to an accounting of costs (which itself may not be that simple, as discussed in Chapter 11). A true analysis of cost-minimization requires firm evidence of outcome equivalency, whether through established literature or from parallel clinical trials (Drummond et al., 1997). Only then should treatment costs be compared, thereby identifying the treatment associated with the lower cost, albeit with the same likelihood of producing the intended therapeutic outcome.

Only when equivalency of outcomes can be scientifically defended should cost-minimization analysis be applied.

COST-MINIMIZATION EXAMPLES

As with the other types of pharmacoeconomic analyses, perhaps the best way to understand cost-minimization analysis is to examine examples of published literature on such research. This section provides examples of appropriate use of cost-minimization analysis; readers are encouraged to explore additional examples on their own.

Agents for Perfusion Imaging

Two vasodilator agents, adenosine and dipyridamole, for myocardial perfusion imaging by single-photon emission computed tomography (SPECT) were compared for their respective levels of cost (Hilleman et al., 1997). For this analysis, the sensitivity and specificity of these two agents were assumed to be equivalent (an assumption that should always be supported). Patients' records were retrospectively examined for a list of predefined costs; inclusion of treatment costs for adverse events allowed differences in safety to be addressed apart from the basic assumption of outcome equivalence. Although adenosine had a higher cost of acquisition, its lower total costs—including lower costs for adverse events associated with treatment—identified adenosine as the preferred vasodilator agent, over dipyridamole, for myocardial perfusion imaging.

Endomysial Antibody for Celiac Disease

A variation on cost-minimization analysis compared strategies of screening tools for celiac disease, a disorder in the absorptive function of the intestine (Atkinson et al., 1997). Biopsy of the small bowel served as the standard for endomysial antibody as an experimental technique. Diagnostic equivalency was assumed, but the 64 percent specificity of endomysial antibody for celiac disease appropriately required sensitivity analysis (as described in Chapter 12). Overall, the least costly diagnostic strategy involved initial screening with endomysial antibody, substantiated by biopsy for those patients testing positive. As might be expected, this result depended upon the level of specificity of the endomysial antibody technique.

Fetal Monitoring in High-Risk Pregnancies

Societal pressure to reduce health care costs often supports strategies for home care, rather than inpatient hospitalization, whenever possible, but this treatment shifting must not be circumvented by additional safety risks. A Dutch study investigated such a shift strategy for home or inpatient location of fetal monitoring for women with high-risk pregnancy (Birnie et al., 1997). With neonatal safety the main outcome measure, this cost-minimization analysis prospectively depended on safety equivalence, with results again tested in sensitivity analysis (see Chapter 12). Both locations of fetal monitoring proved equivalently safe. Moreover, the halving of costs for home monitoring bolstered adoption of this practice for women with high-risk pregnancy.

Pharmacologic Treatment of Depression

As in the previous example, treatment of depression can be shifted to outpatient settings, in this case through the use of new pharmacologic agents. Two such drugs, paroxetine and imipramine, formed the comparison within a cost-minimization analysis that appropriately included tests of outcome equivalency (Melton et al., 1997). Total direct costs (i.e., those linked to the disease and treatment, as described in Chapter 11) were essentially the same; thus, neither drug captured a cost-minimization advantage. Importantly, sources of drug-associated costs differed: paroxetine itself costing more for acquisition; imipramine incurring more expenditures from hospitalization of patients. The relevance of expenditure sources to pharmacoeconomic analysis forms the crux of cost considerations from different perspectives (as detailed in Chapter 9), such as that of the health care provider reimbursing for outpatient drug costs or the institution caring for hospitalized patients.

Antibiotics for Intraabdominal Infections

The institution providing care provided the perspective for a cost-minimization analysis of ampicillin-sulbactam and cefoxitin as two antibiotics for treating hospitalized patients with intra-abdominal infection (Messick et al., 1998). In fact, cost-minimization was only employed after testing equivalency of predefined primary outcomes, including rates of cure and failure, incidence of new infections, and adverse events related to the antibiotic treatments. Under this assumption, the beta-lactamase inhibitor combination of ampicillin-sulbactam had lower costs of drug acquisition than did the cephalosporin cefoxitin. Extending this initial comparison into a cost-effectiveness analysis to include the observed 9 percent greater rate of treatment failure with cefoxitin further supported use of the combination agent for intra-abdominal infections. Hence, cost-minimization analysis may serve as an independent tool or as a specialty technique, depending on outcomes and their degree of equivalence.

Cost-minimization analysis can be used in proven cases of outcome equivalency, or within wider pharmacoeconomic analyses.

Evaluation II

Pharmacoeconomic Analyses

Have you comprehended the differences among the five types of pharmacoeconomic analyses covered in Part II? To check, choose the most appropriate type of analysis for each of the five following scenarios. Then compare your choices, along with your reasons for these choices, with the answers at the end of this section. For follow-up study, review the relevant chapters noted in these answers.

QUESTIONS

1. Two antibiotics have the same rates of eradication for a bacterium of interest in hospital-acquired pneumonia. Both drugs display equivalent safety profiles; one drug, however, requires twice the daily dose of the other. Does either give the health care practitioner a better choice in prescribing for the hospitalized patient who contracts this type of nosocomial pneumonia?

2. With demographics indicating a growing sector of elderly persons in our population, chronic illnesses—such as hypertension—increasingly draw from a finite pool of financial resources. Treatment of borderline hypertension may have positive societal outcomes in the long-term. A plethora of drug treatments are available, but diet with exercise may also be an

option for many patients. Which approach should be taken for a middle-aged person without other complicating factors?

3. Mental illness finally steps from behind a curtain of shame for many patients who face its debilitative effects. Left hidden and untreated, depression can reduce a person's job performance and induce a variety of stress-related disorders. The toll from depression and its associated conditions may be increasing along with the stresses of modern life. Can these costs from depression be tallied to reach an accurate portrayal of this disease's financial drain on society?

4. Despite encouraging results from therapeutic interventions, the many forms of cancer continue to plague modern society. This disease exacts a personal price from the inflicted individuals: not just a shortened lifespan, but also a lower quality of that life, in terms of their physical, emotional, and spiritual pain. For some patients, chemotherapy may prolong life; however, this therapy itself often induces debilitating side effects, such as severe nausea. Can the patient with cancer weigh a chance of longer life against a probability of debilitation?

5. In hospitals and other health care institutions, departments compete for available funds. Just as for society overall, an institution must allocate a finite budget for a seemingly infinite demand for resources. New therapies that have been proven effective and safe will help patients only if funding exists for their implementation and use. If a hospital wants both to implement an influenza vaccination for the elderly and to purchase a more sensitive instrument for magnetic resonance imaging—but has funds for only one—which should be chosen?

ANSWERS

1. *Cost-minimization analysis* would allow the prescriber to choose the antibiotic with the lower cost, since these two drugs are equivalent in efficacy and safety (if this assumption can be defended). Presumably, a lower total dose implies a lower cost, unless a higher acquisition cost offsets this advantage. *(Chapter 8)*

2. *Cost-effectiveness analysis* allows comparison of these different therapies for costs associated with a predefined efficacy measure. This outcome, however, should be quantified as much as possible; for example, a reduction of 5 mmHg in sitting diastolic blood pressure. *(Chapter 6)*

3. *Cost-of-illness analysis*, which focuses on determining the costs attributed to a disease, would apply to this scenario. Indeed, depression exemplifies a case in which this technique can unearth seemingly hidden costs, such as lost time from work and lower productivity when on the job. *(Chapter 4)*

4. *Cost-utility analysis* directly addresses this critical issue of considering quality of life and other subjective outcomes when choosing a treatment for a patient's illness such as cancer. Often, the analysis can provide information with which the patient and physician together can select a suitable therapy *(Chapter 7)*

5. *Cost-benefit analysis* allows comparison of options with disparate objectives, such as these two options of a vaccination program or a diagnostic instrument. By reducing the outcomes to a strictly monetary level, this pharmacoeconomic tool lends itself to budgetary and other policy applications. *(Chapter 5)*

PART III:
TECHNIQUES
OF PHARMACOECONOMIC
RESEARCH

. . . the element of good luck often renders it possible for a physician to give, as it were offhand, diagnoses and prognoses of this exceptional character.

Galen (2nd century A.D.)

Further honing Part II's analysis definitions, Part III examines techniques that render pharmacoeconomic research unique from standard clinical trials.

Chapter 9

Perspectives for Research Analyses

Answers to pharmacoeconomic queries depend not only on the acquired data, but also on the perspective of the research.

Armed with an understanding of the five main types of pharmacoeconomic analyses (as detailed in Part II), we now progress to a discussion of the underlying techniques of pharmacoeconomic research. Of these, perhaps the most fundamental is *perspective:* From whose vantage point do we consider the research, including the costs and outcomes of any medical intervention?

A particularly elegant metaphor of perspective—not for pharmacoeconomics in particular—was developed in the late 1800s by Edwin A. Abbott, a Victorian scholar and theologian of England. Abbott's philosophical novel, *Flatland: A Romance of Many Dimensions* (1884) took readers on a geometric tour through worlds of one, two, and three dimensions, as told from the perspective of an actual square. The protagonist's perspective on any other dimensions depended on filtering perceptions through two-dimensional eyes.

For example, a sphere who inhabited a three-dimensional world passed through the two-dimensional plane of Flatland; the square, however, originally perceived the sphere only as a point that progressively waxed and waned in circles, ending again as a point before disappearing altogether. When the square opened his two-dimensional eyes to the possibility of three dimensions, he began to envision the true nature of the sphere, as well as of dimensions or perspectives different from his own.

We, too, must open our eyes to the different perspectives from which studies in pharmacoeconomics can be designed, written, and interpreted. This chapter provides an overview of the main types of perspectives for pharmacoeconomic research.

PERSPECTIVES FOR PHARMACOECONOMICS

The perspective of a pharmacoeconomic study, whether of a drug or other type of medical intervention, establishes the context for the research. In essence, a study's perspective determines which types of outcome measures (see Chapter 10) and which categories of cost (see Chapter 11) are relevant and meaningful. A health care insurer, for example, would be interested in costs covered by a patient's insurance plan, but not necessarily costs external to the policy. The patient most definitely would focus on the uncovered or out-of-pocket expenditures, whereas a hospital would only note billable expenditures. And society overall might view all of these—and more.

Perspective, then, captures the viewpoints of those making health care decisions (Davidoff and Powe, 1996). The four perspective Ps are the *patient* receiving therapy, the *provider* of services, the *payor* who covers expenditures, and the *public* affected by such issues (see Table 9.1). In each perspective category, different issues take precedence over others. Hence, defining perspective at the outset of a pharmacoeconomic study (see Chapter 13) remains crucial to obtaining useful results.

The perspective taken in pharmacoeconomic research determines the study's design and analysis, as well as its interpretation.

TABLE 9.1. Relevant Issues by Perspective

Perspective	Relevant issues
Patient	Which therapeutic option works best for me?
	What costs must I pay myself?
	How will I feel if I subject myself to this therapy?
Provider	How will my patient fare with the chosen therapy?
	Will the patient's insurance cover these expenditures?
	Will the patient be compliant with this treatment?
Payor	Which treatments should we cover in our formulary?
	How do we adjust actuarial tables for high-risk groups?
	How do legislation and lawsuits affect our decisions?
Public	Will our tax base handle costs for the indigent?
	Does this disease decrease worker productivity?
	Could we better expend our limited funds for other uses?

SCENARIOS OF PERSPECTIVE

Consider these two hypothetical scenarios illustrating the role of perspective in pharmacoeconomic research.

Hypertension, or high blood pressure, can lead to a variety of health disorders, not the least of which is premature death. Today's busy executives find themselves at risk for hypertension because of their age, diet, and lifestyle. Should a middle-aged executive with diagnosed hypertension of a mild-to-moderate degree receive a quick-fix pill, or first be required to modify diet, increase exercise, and reduce stress?

From the perspective of the executive *(patient)*, the quick-fix would be preferred because it does not intrude into an already hectic lifestyle. The executive's family care doctor *(provider)* may not have a preference for either option, as long as the executive's blood pressure improves. The executive's insurance carrier *(payor)*, however, may insist on first trying the option with no financial costs (i.e., lifestyle changes). Society *(public)* must weigh short-term savings of lifestyle changes against long-term costs if the noncompliant executive dies prematurely: decreased contributions in the workplace and increased economic and emotional tolls on surviving family members.

Chronic fatigue syndrome remains a questionable disorder in some corners of health care, while being firmly established as legitimate among many physicians and researchers. A seemingly healthy young adult continues to lose several days of work each month from sheer exhaustion; when able to work, this individual considers his or her efforts substandard. Today's drug armamentarium still lacks any agreed treatments for this person's illness. To what level of care is this young adult with a lifetime's potential entitled?

The young adult *(patient)* will probably accept any treatment that may help. A nurse practitioner *(provider)* may suggest an experimental drug being researched for chronic fatigue syndrome, but the insurer *(payor)* might not reimburse for a drug not yet approved by the FDA. Society *(public)* has much to lose if young adults are unable to contribute to their potential over forty to fifty years of a career. But can society afford to pay for a drug to treat a still controversial condition?

In both scenarios, any of the four main perspectives can be taken; indeed, each sheds its own shade of light from the full spectrum of pharmacoeconomics (see Figure 9.1). Even when a pharmacoeconomic study correctly declares its perspective at the outset, consideration of other viewpoints increases robustness of the research.

Each type of perspective adds to better understanding of the intricacies of pharmacoeconomic research.

REPERCUSSIONS OF PERSPECTIVE

Perspective, then, remains critical to dissemination and use of information from pharmacoeconomic studies. Defining the target

FIGURE 9.1. Perspectives on Pharmacoeconomic Studies

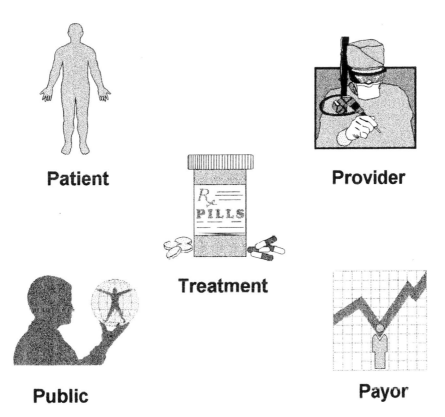

audience for a study's findings allows researchers to select the perspective (or perspectives) most appropriate for decisions by information users. Furthermore, a clearly defined perspective engenders specific objectives and outcome measures that togeth er build a pharmacoeconomic study less vulnerable to unintentional misinterpretation by the target audience. Clear and concise language particularly helps to circumvent this potential problem with dissemination and use of pharmacoeconomic information (Szucs and Mantovani, 1997).

Perspective, though, also raises critical issues on the use of pharmacoeconomic information. Specifically, do results of a pharmacoeconomic study directly apply at the level of the individual patient? Pharmacoeconomic research often pertains to analyses of current or proposed elements of health care policy. Aggregate decisions at the *public* or *payor* levels, however, require the human touch when *provider* and *patient* together reach individual treatment decisions (Asch and Hershey, 1995).

Hence, perspective reinforces a critical issue of health care: Always remember that each patient is an individual with body, heart, and soul, not merely a statistic with disease, insurance, and wallet. The following chapters explicate these repercussions of perspective in pharmacoeconomic research.

Despite key information relevant at the levels of provider, payor, and public, pharmacoeconomic research must always remember that the patient is a person.

Chapter 10

Determination of Outcome Measures

How are outcomes of pharmacoeconomic research measured and interpreted, with consideration of both perspective and type of analysis?

With the appropriate perspective determined, a pharmacoeconomic study must next focus on agents of comparison, along with the basis for their comparison. Which of many drugs, for example, should be evaluated? Do nontraditional approaches, such as meditation, play a role in quality-of-life assessments? How can outcomes related to efficacy, safety, and preference be quantified? At what level will agents be deemed similar or different in outcome? When does a primary outcome take precedence over outcomes of secondary or tertiary importance?

Rather than prescribing specific agents and measures by disease, this chapter provides an overview of the issues underlying the myriad choices available for outcome measures in pharmacoeconomic research.

ALTERNATIVES FOR CLINICAL DECISIONS

As outlined in Part II, each of the five main types of pharmacoeconomic analyses apply to specific situations. All but cost-of-illness analysis involve assessment of treatments; therefore, this chapter focuses on the remaining four types of pharmaco-

economic research. Figure 10.1 diagrams steps in refining outcome measures: first considering the clinical setting or disease
state, next identifying alternative agents relevant to that situation,
and finally reviewing potential outcome measures through the
study's perspective.

To a large extent, the clinical setting or disease state determines
key measures for outcomes. Diet modification versus diuretic
agents for hypertension, for example, could be assessed in terms of
the degree to which each lowers a patient's blood pressure. But
should the research also consider longer-term effects of more importance, such as risk for stroke or other cardiovascular events?
Inclusion of other secondary outcomes also influences a study's
design: changes in blood pressure may be found in weeks or
months, whereas risk of stroke may not become apparent for years
or decades. Hence, researchers must consider issues of practicabil-
ity in defining alternatives and outcomes for a pharmacoeconomic
study.

FIGURE 10.1. Refinement of Outcome Measures

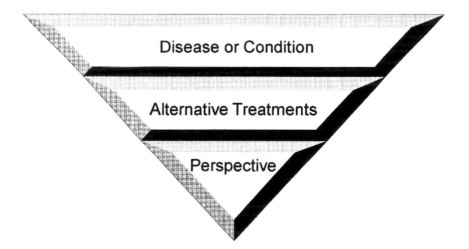

The selection of alternatives for comparison, however, may become even more complicated. For a cost-benefit analysis, the alternatives may not even be for the same disease or use; a hospital, for example, may be assessing whether to hire more nurses or to implement bar-coding in its pharmacy. But when the study directly compares two or more therapies (one of which could be "no treatment" or placebo), researchers must be sure to include those alternatives that are both realistic and available; moreover, the range of choices must encompass not just one typically used, such as a preferred drug class, but also others relevant in that clinical situation, such as psychotherapy. Without careful consideration of alternatives, researchers may inadvertently introduce bias into an otherwise sound analysis (Luce and Elixhauser, 1996).

The selected alternatives may then facilitate further refinement of the proposed outcome measures. Comparison of two drugs of different classes, for instance, may be posited upon a basic assessment of effectiveness, such as eradication of bacteria by a newer or by an older generation of cephalosporin antibiotics. In contrast, comparison of daily exercise and liposuction surgery for treating obesity might require assessments beyond weight reduction: cardiovascular benefits and patient compliance with exercise; surgical complications and weight regain after liposuction.

As a third factor, a study's perspective (see Chapter 9) determines final selection of appropriate outcome measures. Quality of life and other subjective parameters may be of more interest to a patient selecting among alternative treatments, whereas an insurer may focus on primary measures of effectiveness and safety. Perspective thus winnows down the list of outcome measures to those relevant for that research.

Hence, each pharmacoeconomic situation must be viewed within its clinical and research contexts. In this manner, the analysis reflects the disease or application, its treatments or other alternatives, and the research perspective that together determine the relevant outcome measures.

Perspective exerts a controlling force in determining not just study design, but also appropriate outcome measures.

DELINEATION OF OUTCOME MEASURES

From a bewildering array of potential outcome measures, how can researchers of pharmacoeconomics possibly select the few most relevant to the analysis at hand? Specific selection by disease, population, and perspective lie outside the scope of this overview (but may be found by consulting sources noted in Chapter 15). Guidelines on their categorization, though, assist researchers in delineating outcome measures.

The term "health index" typically encompasses outcome measures that describe or quantify not just physical, but also social, emotional, and well-being functions (Boyer et al., 1998). Linked by their goal of expressing health as a multidimensional construct, health-index techniques can vary: one parameter or a composite score; one point or extended time frames; and one patient or population groups. Complexity also varies: from yes/no scores of death or survival to morbidities related to disease progression; from objective ratings measured by observers to subjective scales indicated by the patients themselves. And with recognition of the interrelatedness of body and spirit will come even broader indices of health. However, the need of pharmacoeconomic research to quantify ratios of costs to outcomes introduces the often problematic issue of weighting dimensions by the importance of their contribution to the overall scale.

Viewed from a different angle, outcome measures can further be categorized by whether they act explicitly on a patient's physical, social, or emotional state; use more or less health care or other resources; or affect a patient's quality of life (Drummond et al., 1997). Explicit outcomes refer to those health indices already described; resource consumption and quality of life, however, require further elaboration (see Table 10.1).

Resource use, in fact, remains controversial in pharmacoeconomics. Resource consumption can be broken down into two subdivisions. First are resources directly relating to the disease or treatment, whether consumed by the patient or by the patient's family or other intimates. For example, does a surgical treatment consume more resources in the hospital or long-term care facility while giving a needed respite to the patient's parents, spouse, or children? Perspective indeed enters into such an equation (see Chapter 9).

In addition to these direct uses of resources, indirect consumption of resources in the form of decreased social productivity must be considered. For instance, patients who lose more time from work theoretically contribute less than their potential to society's

TABLE 10.1. Categorization of Outcome Measures

Category of outcome	Examples of outcome measures
Explicit health indices	*Physical states,* such as death, disability, or pain
	Social functions, such as interacting with family members
	Emotional manifestations, such as anxiety or depression
Resource consumption	*Directly by patient,* as for drugs or physical therapy
	Directly by others, as for home care provided by family
	Indirectly by patient, as for lost time from employment
	Indirectly by others, as for decreased work productivity
Quality of life	*General assessments,* such as satisfaction with life
	Specific assessments, such as sleep or sexual function

composite productivity, and caregivers also stand to lose on these indirect measurements. Arguably, valuation of an individual's contribution to society introduces not just mathematical complexity, but also philosophical conundrums, rendering indirect outcomes problematic at best. (Chapter 14 further explores such ethical issues within pharmacoeconomic research.)

Finally, subjective outcomes, notably quality of life, must be addressed. These outcomes form the crux primarily of cost-utility analyses (see Chapter 7), but may also be included secondarily as measures in the other types of pharmacoeconomic research. Quality-of-life assessments in particular represent their own field of expertise. The multiple dimensions that make up quality of life, along with the variety of tools for their measurement, must be carefully selected, with key statistical attributes, such as variability and reliability, appropriately considered (Testa and Nackley, 1994).

Despite the inherent complexity, outcome measures provide pharmacoeconomic researchers with a breadth and depth of assessments through which to quantify results of drugs, programs, or other therapeutic interventions. Coupling these outcomes with appropriate cost categories (as described in Chapter 12) builds an analysis meeting the objectives of the planned pharmacoeconomic research.

The wide range of available outcome measures can be categorized by their relationships to patients and those who provide their care.

Chapter 11

Categorization
of Pharmacoeconomic Costs

How are pharmacoeconomic costs categorized and interpreted, particularly from the vantage of research perspective?

Unlike measurement of outcomes (as discussed in Chapter 10), categorization of *costs*—often termed "expenditures"—does not explicitly depend on the specific type of pharmacoeconomic analysis being performed. Instead, costs provide a commonality across these research types: despite their different outcomes component, all analyses include some quantification of cost. Of more importance to understanding the basics of pharmacoeconomics are the categories of costs and the methods for calculating them for any of the five main types of analysis (as described in Part II).

Hence, this chapter explores the measurement of costs across the various types of pharmacoeconomic research, focusing not only on categories of costs, but also on problematic issues in their assessment.

KEY CATEGORIES OF COSTS

Costs in pharmacoeconomic research fall into four basic categories (see Table 11.1), stratified by two parameters: directly or indirectly related to the disease, treatment, or program; and medical or nonmedical in nature. The following delineation of these

TABLE 11.1. Examples of Categorized Costs

Relationship to disease, treatment, or program	Nature of cost or expenditure	
	Medical	**Nonmedical**
Direct	*Direct medical costs:* Hospital fees, drugs, equipment, supplies, and professional fees	*Direct nonmedical costs:* Transportation for care, lodging for family, and additional home care
Indirect	*Indirect medical costs:* Earnings lost during illness or treatment, and from disability	*Indirect nonmedical costs:* Intangible effects, such as quality of life, and psychological tolls

Sources: Adapted from Drummond et al., 1997b, and Larson, 1996.

four categories of costs applies across all types of pharmacoeconomic analyses.

Direct medical costs include those expenditures that result from the illness or intervention, and that are clinical or therapeutic in nature. A patient undergoing surgery in an outpatient setting, for example, would incur costs for clinic time, doctor and nurse fees, drugs and pharmacy supplies, and equipment use. In contrast, a patient hospitalized for surgery would additionally face costs for "room and board" while an inpatient.

Direct nonmedical costs represent expenditures attributable to the illness or intervention, but not of a clinical or therapeutic nature. A patient with cancer requiring daily radiation treatments would expend funds for transportation to the facility; if distant, the therapy site might require lodging costs for the patient and family, and perhaps care for the home in their absence during treatment periods.

Indirect medical costs reflect a level of expenditures not immediately apparent: lost earnings or lower productivity of the patient because of the illness or intervention, or from long-term or permanent disability. A patient unable to work while recuperating from severe pneumonia or a car accident, as examples, might lose wages during this period; if compensated, the patient would not lose money, but the policy carrier for the patient's medical insurance would. *Note the influence of perspective in this situation*—lost wages compensated by insurance would not be included in a pharmacoeconomic analysis from the patient's perspective, but would be from the payor's perspective.

Indirect nonmedical costs include effects somewhat removed from the illness or intervention. A patient with schizophrenia, for instance, not only incurs costs from all three of the previous categories, but also faces a huge toll in terms of inability to function in society, decreased happiness or life quality, and a variety of psychological demons. Again, perspective plays a pivotal role, since these "intangible costs" may be more relevant to the patient, provider, and public than to a payor whose defined responsibility lies outside this wider scope.

Given these four categories of costs, how does a researcher decide upon those appropriate to the planned pharmacoeconomic analysis? Primarily by its *perspective* (see Chapter 9 for details on the four main types of perspective.) The examples above give an inkling of the perspective points to be considered in selecting cost categories; the next section raises additional issues that can complicate cost calculations.

Inclusion of different categories of costs depends more upon perspective than on the specific type of analysis.

ISSUES IN CALCULATING COSTS

Even after determining the appropriate cost categories for a pharmacoeconomic analysis according to its predefined perspective, the researcher confronts another key hurdle: how are these costs actually calculated? Techniques often depend on the cost category itself. Direct medical costs, for instance, can be found as market prices or as actual fees for products or services. Of course, these also vary by individual provider, time period, and geographic area; such variation must be addressed or at least clearly acknowledged in the research reports (as discussed in Chapter 13). Moreover, indirect costs challenge researchers even more, since the value attached to a patient's quality of life does not easily reduce to pure economic terms (see Chapter 14).

Irrespective of these initial stumbling blocks, the researcher must next determine the specific types or subcategories of costs for the analysis. Of these types, the three most common are *total, average,* and *marginal* costs (Pindyck and Rubinfeld, 1997), each representing a different element of expenditures for an item or service (see Table 11.2). (See Chapter 15 for sources of detailed information on cost structures.)

To illustrate distinctions and potential uses among these types of costs, consider the example of a van that brings mammography screening to low-income areas. *Total costs* of screening for breast cancer with this program include the van and equipment, gasoline and maintenance, and technician fees and services. Of these costs, the van and the mammography equipment represent

TABLE 11.2. Types of Pharmacoeconomic Costs

Type of cost	Definition*
Total cost	Sum of all expenditures related to a product or service, including:
	fixed costs that do not change with each unit of output, and *variable costs* that relate to the specific level of production
Average cost	Expenditure for a level of output, divided by the number of units
Marginal cost	Incremental expenditure to produce one additional unit of output

Source: Adapted from Pindyck and Rubinfeld, 1997.

fixed costs of outlay that do not change in the short-term provision of this program. *Variable costs* include not just transportation expenditures for each trip, but also the technical time and supplies consumed with each mammography. From the perspective of the hospital or clinic providing this service, all of these costs are relevant. But running a service over several years introduces a key issue of fixed costs: should they be charged only to the first year of the program, evenly averaged over the full years of service, or accounted for by capital depreciation? Next, should the payor or public funding this service for the indigent focus on *average costs* of each mammography? Or on the *marginal or incremental cost* of providing one extra mammography? (And this example does not even address the indirect medical costs, if any, of those coming for mammography screening, or, more to the point, the intangible costs associated with the worry of being diagnosed.)

Two remaining issues for calculating costs—*inflation* and *discounting*—relate to time (Drummond et al., 1997a). *Inflation* of costs logically exerts greater force in any pharmacoeconomic analyses extended over years, particularly if certain specific costs (e.g., physician fees or prescription drugs) would be expected to increase more steeply than other items in the general economy. Otherwise, inflation can often be precluded as an important issue in calculating costs.

Discounting, in some respects, represents the reverse of inflation: costs incurred in the present carry greater weight than costs incurred in the future because of different perceptions over time. Although seemingly confusing, discounting can be understood with the analogy of winning a lottery: a lump sum today appears more valuable than a monthly payment over a lifetime. Except for extremely short-term interventions focusing on immediate costs, pharmacoeconomic analyses must address discounting.

Specific methods to address such discounting, as well as other assumptions and uncertainties in pharmacoeconomic research, stand outside the scope of this overview (but can be explored through sources listed in Chapter 15). However, the fundamental principle involved, termed *sensitivity analysis*, forms the topic of the next chapter.

Calculation of pharmacoeconomic costs must consider not only the kinds of costs, but also the time frame over which costs are incurred.

Chapter 12

Sensitivity Analysis of Assumptions

How does sensitivity analysis of assumptions and uncertainties strengthen all types of pharmacoeconomic research?

Research perspectives. Outcome measures. Cost categories. Each of these topics from the earlier chapters of Part III raises issues surrounding uncertainty and the assumptions required in pharmacoeconomic analyses. Despite such issues, reliability of studies can be augmented through testing the degree to which assumptions, values, and uncertainties affect research results. This chapter covers the key technique of these important elements of pharmacoeconomic research: sensitivity analysis.

RATIONALE FOR SENSITIVITY ANALYSIS

Controlled circumstances, standard practice for sound scientific research, often elude pharmacoeconomic analysis. After all, increased control of the research environment decreases the generalizability of results to the wider health care population (Chapter 3). Moreover, ethical mores constrain the variations of health care decisions in studies that involve humans as patients and providers, with legal and regulatory issues delimiting the overall environment for involvement of payors and the public (Chapter 14).

As emphasized in Chapter 9, the perspective(s) of the pharmacoeconomic study must be decided at the outset, thereby defining outcomes measures (Chapter 10) and cost categories (Chapter 11). But what degree of vagary remains in determining these parameters, even with a predefined perspective? Furthermore, do the data measured in the study, or obtained from published or commercial sources, themselves contribute to variability of the study's results?

For example, consider a pharmacoeconomic study hypothetically assessing the relative merits of prenatal care. Ethically, researchers cannot withhold such care from expectant women simply for scientific control. Instead, epidemiological or statistical data for certain populations could be accessed. If these sources lacked the originally desired parameters, such as dietary consumption, then the researchers would adjust the study, perhaps using anecdotal reports of "daily servings of fruits and vegetables" instead of precise percentages of recommended nutrients.

And costs? Actual expenditures of the women, their insurance carriers, and any supplemental agents might not be available. Government statistics on consumer prices and inflation might need to be substituted. A trickier issue would be assigning a monetary value to any changes in physical or intellectual prowess of the study's infants, as would be appropriate for a public or societal perspective.

Because of these issues in pharmacoeconomic research, sensitivity analysis is typically employed (Luce and Elixhauser, 1996). This cluster of techniques allows researchers to stress the study's design. Assumptions and values are varied within reasonable bounds, with effects of these uncertainties quantified as possible. This approach allows researchers to measure the soundness of their conclusions: little or no effect suggests low sensitivity to the parameter varied; a greater effect shows limitations to the study's conclusions. An overview of sensitivity techniques follows.

Sensitivity analysis allows researchers to test limitations to the generalizability of pharmacoeconomic findings.

METHODS FOR TESTING SENSITIVITY

Specific methods for testing sensitivity depend on the outcome measures and cost categories used in the pharmacoeconomic study. Rather than dissecting a limited number of these techniques, this section reviews the general methodological approach for sensitivity analysis. Chapter 15 recommends sources for detailed information on such techniques.

The overall approach to the various techniques of sensitivity analysis uses three basic steps, each with issues to be considered within a pharmacoeconomic study (Drummond et al., 1997). *Step 1* involves identifying assumptions, parameters, or methods subject to uncertainty; examples include outcomes for investigational drugs, list prices rather than actual charges, and predicted rates of inflation or discounting. *Step 2* places upper and lower bounds on assumptions so that repeated analyses can assess effects of expected and reasonable variation; sources of these bounds include evidence from other studies, commercial or published compendiums of relevant data, and informed opinions from decision makers. *Step 3* then requires that results of repeated calculations be reinterpreted to determine if the varied parameter affects the study's conclusions; minimally, this step involves using the most reasonable or "best-guess" value, along with "least and most conservative" values for that parameter. Table 12.1 also provides a list of questions in sensitivity analysis.

As perhaps to be expected in a relatively young field like pharmacoeconomics, the use of strengthening techniques like sensitivity analysis must mature along with the research itself. A review of ninety-three pharmacoeconomic studies published during 1992, for instance, found that only slightly more than one-third reported adequate information on sensitivity analysis of uncertainty (Briggs and Sculpher, 1995). Increased awareness on the part of critical readers of published pharmacoeconomic studies, however, will foster higher standards for the conduct of this key technique of research.

TABLE 12.1. Questions in Sensitivity Analysis

Study parameter	Typical questions in sensitivity analysis
Research perspective	Does the study's perspective match the target audience?
	Which additional perspective(s) should be considered?
	How do conclusions change with another perspective?
Outcome measures	Do the measurements capture all outcomes of interest?
	How much variation could reasonably be expected?
	Would conclusions change if this variation did occur?
Cost categorization	Have all appropriate cost categories been included?
	How variable are estimates of inflation and discounting?
	Do conclusions change with different cost estimations?

The remaining chapters of this book (Part IV) explore such issues for proper evaluation of pharmacoeconomic information.

Critical awareness of sensitivity analysis promotes development of methods for this backbone of pharmacoeconomic research.

Evaluation III

Pharmacoeconomic Techniques

Have you understood the key messages of Part III? To check, answer these questions. Then compare your answers with those at the end of this section. For follow-up study, review the relevant chapters noted in these answers.

QUESTIONS

1. Pharmacoeconomic studies can take on changing meanings when viewed from different vantages or perspectives. List and define the four types of perspectives in pharmacoeconomic research.

2. Outcome measures, which assess how well a program or intervention functions, can be categorized according to their relationship to the patient and the patient's caregivers. List the three broad categories of outcome measures, with an example of each type.

3. Unlike outcome measures, categories of costs or expenditures depend less on a specific pharmacoeconomic analysis and more on a study's perspective. What are the two main parameters by which costs can be categorized? Name the four resulting categories, with an example of each.

4. Because costs associated with a disease, treatment, or other intervention occur over time, pharmacoeconomic studies of

considerable duration must assess the effects of inflation and discounting. Compare and contrast these two terms.

5. Sensitivity analysis allows researchers to test the strength of pharmacoeconomic research. What are the three main steps common to any sensitivity analysis?

ANSWERS

1. The four Ps of pharmacoeconomic perspectives are the *patient* receiving care, the *provider* of that care, the *payor* covering expenditures, and the overall *public* affected by health care decisions. The perspective(s) of a pharmacoeconomic study determine its design, analysis, and interpretation. *(Chapter 9)*

2. Despite inherent variety, outcome measures can be generally divided into *explicit health indices,* including physical states such as death, social functions such as relationships, and emotional manifestations such as anxiety; *resource consumption,* including drugs, home care, lost work time, and decreased productivity; and *quality of life,* including general assessments of life satisfaction and specific assessments of sleep or other functions. *(Chapter 10)*

3. Pharmacoeconomic costs can be stratified by the directness of their relationship to the disease or intervention, and by their nature being medical or nonmedical. From this two-level stratification come four cost categories: *direct medical costs,* such as hospital and professional fees; *direct nonmedical costs,* such as lodging for the family during a patient's offsite treatment; *indirect medical costs,* such as earnings lost from disability; and *indirect nonmedical or intangible costs,* such as various psychological tolls on the patient or the patient's family. *(Chapter 11)*

4. In some respects, inflation and discounting represent opposite issues in assessing the effects of time on pharmacoeconomic studies. Inflation accounts for changes in costs due to the general economic climate, whereas discounting refers to decreases in perceived values for future occurrences. *(Chapter 11)*

5. Sensitivity analysis generally occurs in three steps: (1) identifying assumptions that are subject to uncertainty; (2) placing reasonable bounds on variation; and (3) interpreting results of repeat analyses. Increased awareness of the importance of sensitivity analysis will continue to strengthen this pivotal technique of pharmacoeconomic research. *(Chapter 12)*

PART IV:
EVALUATION
OF PHARMACOECONOMIC
INFORMATION

Life is short, science is long; opportunity is elusive, experience is dangerous, judgment is difficult.

Hippocrates (4th-5th century B.C.)

As pharmacoeconomic data are collected and reported, a discerning eye is necessary for evaluating the information. Part IV offers such guidance.

Chapter 13

Review of Pharmacoeconomic Research

Across pharmacoeconomic analyses, what are the major evaluation factors that reflect thorough and sound results?

In Part IV, all aspects of pharmacoeconomic research come together. Parts I, II, and III introduced and elaborated on pharmacoeconomic basics, analysis types, and research techniques, respectively. The qualitative, not quantitative, approach focuses on fostering understanding of pharmacoeconomics and outcomes research, rather than on conducting studies themselves.

Nonetheless, readers of pharmacoeconomic research must exercise discretion in evaluating the burgeoning reports in today's literature. This chapter synthesizes key points from earlier chapters into steps and evaluation factors for pharmacoeconomic research; the next chapter raises issues of regulatory and ethical concern; and the final chapter recommends sources for readers who wish to delve deeper into the field of pharmacoeconomics.

STEPS IN PHARMACOECONOMIC RESEARCH

Steps common to various types of pharmacoeconomic analyses can be found in several research publications, including those cited in support of specific analysis types in Part II, and the research techniques addressed in Part III. The following steps build upon these sources, but with a particular focus on understanding and evaluating—not conducting—pharmacoeconomic research. This shortened, seven-step list combines related substeps that target the writer and reader, rather than only the researcher, of pharmacoeconomic information.

Step 1: *Define the study objective and research perspective.* What specifically does this study endeavor to determine? From which of the four main perspectives will the study be conducted, and its results interpreted?

Step 2: *Identify any alternative agents and their methods of comparison.* Does this study involve a comparison of all relevant alternatives for treatment? Do the methods of comparison reflect the clinical situation and its therapies?

Step 3: *Measure outcomes as appropriate to the analysis type.* What are the main outcomes measurements in this therapeutic situation? Do the measures in this study agree with the study objective and research perspective?

Step 4: *Value cost categories appropriate to the perspective.* Which cost categories should be included in this study? Are inflation, discounting, and any related issues addressed in these calculations?

Step 5: *Calculate summations and ratios of costs versus outcomes.* Were costs and outcomes meaningfully summed? How were ratios of costs to outcomes calculated for the type of analysis used in the study?

Step 6: *Conduct sensitivity analysis of research assumptions.* Which assumptions or calculations inherently introduce uncertainty into the research? Were these assumptions tested for their impact on the study's findings?

Step 7: *Interpret and disseminate the findings of the research study.* What do these findings mean in the context of study objectives and research perspectives? How can these findings be effectively communicated?

Although seemingly obvious, this last step of disseminating the research findings emphasizes the critical nature of *communication* within the wider medical community. The findings of excellent research—be they positive, neutral, or negative in relation to the study's objective—can only benefit the patient, provider, payor, and public when communicated in useful formats and through effective media. Factors in evaluating the disseminated research findings follow in the next section.

Critical readers of pharmacoeconomic findings must themselves understand the main steps common to the various analysis types.

FACTORS IN RESEARCH EVALUATION

Complementing the steps above, factors in the evaluation of pharmacoeconomic research assist readers in critiquing reports and publications. Scientists and readers of scientific information rely on publication standards, such as peer review, that safeguard the integrity of findings (Bonk, 1998). Despite occasional lapses, scientific publications generally represent sound research—or, at a minimum, research whose shortcomings have been analyzed, discussed, and presented for readers to assess.

Nonetheless, pharmacoeconomic research may remain subject to insufficiencies in sound evaluation criteria before publications reach the research community. Why? Simply because this field is still young and evolving. Formal courses and professional workshops grow in number and availability, thereby pointing to future improvements in quality. The proliferation of peer-reviewed journals dedicated to pharmacoeconomics (as suggested in Chapter 15) ensures that publication standards will mature.

Even the more general journals in medical research publish pharmacoeconomic reports, however. These medical journals potentially represent important conduits to a wider audience than the pharmacoeconomic specialists targeted by dedicated journals. In the medical journals, lack of clearly defined evaluative criteria for pharmacoeconomic reports has been identified (Jefferson and Demicheli, 1995). Delineation of guidelines and policies for pharmacoeconomic publications, such as for the *New England Journal of Medicine* (Kassirer and Angell, 1994) and *British Medical Journal* (Drummond and Jefferson, 1996) begin to address and, perhaps more important, publicize this key need.

The American College of Physicians tackled this fundamental issue through its Task Force on Principles for Economic Analysis of Health Care Technology (1995). In this forum, representatives from the academic community, the pharmaceutical industry, the public sector, and private research organizations collaboratively developed criteria to foster the integrity of pharmacoeconomic research. Issues relevant to dissemination of research findings follow (with ethical points addressed in the next chapter).

Analysis of research data must be sufficiently comprehensive to ensure that the researcher's particular views do not sway the conclusions. Data should be understandable to the reader; for example, statistical models must be explained, and calculations clarified with examples if necessary. As for other types of research, timely dissemination of findings (regardless of support or contradiction of hypotheses) ensures that others have appropriate access. The current malleability of those methods involved in pharmacoeconomic research further requires inclusion of the rationale underpinning a particular study's design.

In the next chapter, this theme of responsible reporting of pharmacoeconomic findings continues to be developed. Discussion of regulatory and ethical issues highlights the importance of ensuring the integrity of disseminated information in the field of pharmacoeconomics.

Evolving policies and guidelines for pharmacoeconomic publications foster credible research in this developing field.

Chapter 14

Regulatory and Ethical Considerations

How do governmental regulations and ethical issues in drug development apply to pharmacoeconomics?

Pharmacoeconomic research continues to flourish, partly under its own strong momentum. But fundamentally driving this important field are forces of the health care milieu: pharmaceutical companies seeking to differentiate their products; physicians and other practitioners needing to select among treatment options; payors of insurance firms and other carriers managing fiscal constraints; and ultimately patients and the public taking a greater stand as consumers of drugs and other treatments.

Indeed, these forces surrounding modern health care research broaden the types of documents to be created, reviewed, and used—with concomitant responsibilities for those involved in the process (Bonk, 1998). At the same time, governments develop regulations as a mechanism for ensuring that research benefits their citizenry without undue risks. This chapter reviews such regulatory and ethical issues for pharmacoeconomics.

INFLUENCE OF REGULATORY GUIDELINES

As in other areas of health care research, government bodies exert influence, whether directly through formal regulations and guidelines, or indirectly through their oversight of marketing and promotion of pharmaceutical products. Moreover, agencies need time and funds to build their internal expertise in these new areas. The growing development of regulatory influence over pharmacoeconomics, however, highlights the importance of this growing research sphere.

Australia was the first government to issue formal guidelines, originally effective in January, 1993 (Henry, 1992). Through Australia's Pharmaceutical Benefits Advisory Committee, costs and effectiveness both play in decisions about listing new drugs on its formulary, or approved list of treatments. These formal guidelines spotlight issues of value and cost, proffering a model for other government agencies to consider (Langley, 1993). Recommendations for improving what were perceived as restrictive regulations in the original version led to a revised version of the Australian guidelines, effective in November, 1995 (Langley, 1996).

To date, the U.S. Food and Drug Administration (FDA) has not issued guidelines formalizing inclusion of pharmacoeconomic evidence in submissions for marketing approval. But the FDA does encourage pharmaceutical sponsors to review plans for such research. Additional guidelines should evolve, but only in tandem with maturation of the field itself, and with adaptation to the type of health care environment of a given country's health care system.

Development of formal regulations for pharmacoeconomic research must parallel maturation of this evolving field.

ISSUES OF ETHICAL CONCERN

Formal regulatory guidelines notwithstanding, pharmacoeconomic research does raise serious ethical issues for consideration by all those who generate or use its data and findings. Formularies that declare which drugs or treatments will be allowed for those covered by a particular plan (whether government, hospital, or private insurance) should not simply list those products with the cheapest price; instead, formularies must balance costs and outcomes to optimize expenditures for treatments (Sanchez, 1996). Otherwise, appropriate provision of health care to patients—the ultimate aim—may be compromised.

Despite methodological advances, pharmacoeconomic research still relies on data with value and limitations; uncertainty in assumptions surrounding these data thus must be properly assessed within a study's design (Freemantle and Maynard, 1994). Even the timing of studies can affect the results, necessitating periodic reassessment to ensure that pharmacoeconomic information remains relevant as new drugs move from controlled clinical settings in drug development to wider population use in uncontrolled scenarios (Bloom and Fendrick, 1996).

Of paramount concern to the conduct of sound pharmacoeconomic research is the issue of funding. With pharmaceutical companies as the main sponsors of new drug development, influence over study design and data interpretation may unintentionally (or sometimes intentionally) introduce bias into the research. Guidelines for publication of pharmacoeconomic information recommend safeguards to preclude or minimize such bias; these safeguards highlight ensuring independence of the researcher, along with methodological points uniquely germane to this specific field (Task Force on Principles for Economic Analysis of Health Care Technology, 1995).

How do we proceed into this widening vista of pharmacoeconomics? *Accessing* its information through published reports (like those recommended in the final chapter) is not enough. *Assessing* this information commands at least equal importance. Armed with a basic understanding of the fundamentals of pharmacoeconomics, as developed throughout this book, we all must be critical reviewers.

But, as information users, we too have our own ethical responsibility: to carefully review, constructively critique, and astutely implement findings of pharmacoeconomic research. As writers and readers, we represent a unique audience for this information, with our own perspective. And our perspective will only sharpen its focus as we further delve into this new field. Working together with researchers, we, as information users, can collaboratively contribute to the evolution and maturation of this pivotal field called pharmacoeconomics.

As critical readers, we can contribute to the evolution of pharmaco-economic research by sharpening our unique perspective.

Chapter 15

Sources for Pharmacoeconomic Information

Where can writers and readers find more detailed sources of information on pharmacoeconomic research?

Ready to tackle more detailed literature on pharmacoeconomics? This chapter suggests books, journals, and databases as a starting point. Understanding the basic concepts of pharmacoeconomics facilitates advancement to these—and then higher—levels of information. Remember: keep your perspective on pharmacoeconomics.

BOOKS

Principles of Pharmacoeconomics, edited by J. L. Bootman, R. J. Townsend, and W. F. McGhan (1996, Second Edition, Cincinnati, OH: Harvey Whitney Book Company).

This overview of many issues surrounding pharmacoeconomic research provides methodological information on conducting studies, such as decision analysis.

Studies in Pharmaceutical Economics, edited by M. C. Smith (1996, Binghamton, NY: Pharmaceutical Products Press, an imprint of The Haworth Press, Inc.).

This collection comprises information from researchers in pharmacoeconomics. Topics range from analytical techniques to public policy—and everything in between.

Methods for the Economic Evaluation of Health Care Programmes, by M. F. Drummond, B. J. O'Brien, G. L. Stoddart, and G. Torrance (1997, Second Edition, Oxford: Oxford University Press).

More comprehensive in approach, this book tackles in detail the intricacies of pharmacoeconomic techniques, such as sensitivity analysis. Its many examples and literature critiques complement theoretical discussions.

Health Care Economics, by P. J. Feldstein (1998, Fifth Edition, Albany, NY: Delmar Publishers Inc.).

Not focusing on pharmacoeconomics explicitly, this text theoretically explores the wider health care vista. Prices, competition, insurance, and politics represent the expanse of this book's topics.

JOURNALS

PharmacoEconomics (Adis International Limited).

This international journal explores the relationship between economic issues and clinical practice, with a focus on drug therapy and disease management. Although primarily composed of review articles, this journal also covers original research.

Value in Health (Blackwell Sciences, Inc.).

Sponsored by the International Society for Pharmacoeconomics and Outcomes Research, this new journal launched its inaugural volume in May/June 1998. International in scope, this journal focuses on the application of pharmacoeconomics and outcomes research.

Journal of Research in Pharmaceutical Economics (Pharmaceutical Products Press, an imprint of The Haworth Press, Inc.).

This journal reports on research of drug economic analyses, including comparisons with non-drug treatments. Additional topics include issues of public policy and consumer economics.

Health Economics (John Wiley & Sons, Inc.).

More theoretical in approach, this journal tackles evaluation of health and health care within their economic environment. Topics encompass not just pharmacoeconomic research, but also supply and demand, market mechanisms, efficiency of allocation, and equity of systems.

DATABASES

Of various search databases for accessing medical literature, *Internet Grateful Med,* provided gratis by the U.S. National Library of Medicine, represents a particularly fecund route for finding pharmacoeconomic information. The following two databases are of special relevance:

MEDLINE® (MEDlars onLINE) accesses the computerized system MEDLARS® (MEDical Literature Analysis and Retrieval System). This bibliographic repository from at least 3,700 international biomedical journals focuses on medicine and allied health. As these journals publish more pharmacoeconomic studies, MEDLINE will increasingly identify relevant citations.

HealthSTAR (Health Services, Technology, Administration, and Research) trims sources from MEDLINE to those specific to clinical outcomes and health care delivery. Currently encompassing about 2.5 million records (as of 1998), HealthSTAR includes journal articles, government reports, conference abstracts, and book excerpts. With its health care focus, HealthSTAR includes citations not necessarily available in MEDLINE, thereby providing additional access to pharmacoeconomic literature.

Sources for pharmacoeconomic literature encompass books, journals, and databases in both biomedical and specialist genres.

Evaluation IV

Pharmacoeconomic Information

Have you understood the key messages of Part IV? To check, answer these questions. Then compare your answers with those at the end of this section. For follow-up study, review the relevant chapters noted in these answers.

QUESTIONS

1. Users of pharmacoeconomic information must be familiar with the basic steps of this type of research. How does familiarity with research steps contribute to the proper use of pharmacoeconomic information?

2. As an evolving field, pharmacoeconomic research can be unintentionally biased until agreed-upon standards assume more prominence. Describe a few of these risks.

3. Development and marketing of pharmaceutical products is under close scrutiny by regulatory agencies of governments. To what extent do regulations apply to pharmacoeconomic research?

4. Along with those who conduct pharmacoeconomic research, we who use their published information have ethical responsibilities. Describe this responsibility, in terms of *accessing* versus *assessing* pharmacoeconomic information.

5. Pharmacoeconomic information can be found in a variety of biomedical sources, as well as in specialty publications. Why should both genres be checked when searching for pharmacoeconomic information?

ANSWERS

1. Appropriate use of any information type, including pharmacoeconomic research, relies on a reader's ability to critique its value and weigh its shortcomings. As an evolving field, pharmacoeconomics has its own unique techniques, which remain somewhat malleable until firmer standards coalesce. Readers of this information must therefore be sufficiently familiar with the research steps and techniques to foster critical review. *(Chapter 13)*

2. Risks inherent in the evolving field of pharmacoeconomics include the following: data insufficiently broad so that conclusions are swayed in favor of hypotheses; overcomplication of methodological details that preclude understanding a study; and delayed publication that limits timely access of new findings. *(Chapter 13)*

3. Government agencies influence pharmacoeconomic research (as well as other fields) directly through regulations and guidelines that delimit the conduct of studies, as well as indirectly through oversight of marketing and promotional materials. Australia led the way for formal guidelines, with other governments (including the United States) deferring the issue until this evolving field matures. Government agencies, along with researchers and readers, must hone skills in this field before regulations become comprehensively formalized. *(Chapter 14)*

4. *Accessing* information can be done by anyone who can enter a library, whereas *assessing* information necessarily involves

prudent review of not only findings, but also techniques and assumptions underpinning the research. As users of information, we thus carry the ethical onus to understand pharmacoeconomic research, its scientific conduct, and any societal implications. *(Chapter 14)*

5. Pharmacoeconomic studies are conducted not just by economic specialists, but also by biomedical researchers. Hence, publications may appear in either type of genre. Although search databases overlap, review of more than one source of citations benefits users of pharmacoeconomic information. *(Chapter 15)*

References

Chapter 1

Drummond, M. F., B. J. O'Brien, G. L. Stoddart, and G. Torrance. (1997). *Methods for the Economic Evaluation of Health Care Programmes*, Second Edition. See chapter "Basic types of economic evaluation." Oxford: Oxford University Press.

Fuchs, V. R. (1984). The "rationing" of medical care. *New England Journal of Medicine* 311(24):1572-1573.

Chapter 2

Adamcik, B. A. (1997). The consumers of health care. In: *Pharmacy and the U.S. Health Care System,* Second Edition, edited by J. E. Fincham and A. I. Wertheimer. Binghamton, NY: Pharmaceutical Products Press, an imprint of The Haworth Press, Inc.

Bonk, R. J. (1998). *Medical Writing in Drug Development: A Practical Guide for Pharmaceutical Research.* See chapter "Basic introduction to medical writing." Binghamton, NY: Pharmaceutical Products Press, an imprint of The Haworth Press, Inc.

Bonk, R. J., M. J. Myers, C. H. Knowlton, D. Sabapathi, and W. F. McGhan. (1996). Dynamic competition as an exploratory model of healthcare policy for the antihypertensive market. *PharmacoEconomics* 10(3):251-261.

Bonk, R. J., M. J. Myers, and W. F. McGhan. (1995). Drug expenditures in a balanced strategy for healthcare policy. *PharmacoEconomics* 7(6):534-542.

Burner, S. T., D. R. Waldo, and D. R. McKusick. (1992). National health expenditures through the year 2030. *Health Care Financing Review* 14(1):1-29.

Larson, L. N. (1997). Financing health care in the United States. In: *Pharmacy and the U.S. Health Care System*, Second Edition, edited by J. E. Fincham and A. I. Wertheimer. Binghamton, NY: Pharmaceutical Products Press, an imprint of The Haworth Press, Inc.

Levit, K. R., H. C. Lazenby, B. R. Braden, and the National Health Accounts Team. (1998). National health spending trends in 1996. *Health Affairs* 17(1):35-51.

Chapter 3

Arikian, S. R., M. C. Shannon, T. R. Einarson, S. Cohen, and L. M. Cohen. (1992). The demand for pharmacoeconomic research is on the rise. *Medical Marketing and Media* 27:60-67.

Bonk, R. J. (1993). Pharmacoeconomic evaluation to assist prescription drug pricing: A U.S. perspective on an international issue. *PharmacoEconomics* 4(2):73-76.

Bonk, R. J. (1998a). *Medical Writing in Drug Development: A Practical Guide for Pharmaceutical Research.* See chapter "Overview of drug development." Binghamton, NY: Pharmaceutical Products Press, an imprint of The Haworth Press, Inc.

Bonk, R. J. (1998b). *Medical Writing in Drug Development: A Practical Guide for Pharmaceutical Research.* See chapter "Promotional pieces for marketing." Binghamton, NY: Pharmaceutical Products Press, an imprint of The Haworth Press, Inc.

Bootman, J. L., R. J. Townsend, and W. F. McGhan. (1996). Introduction to pharmacoeconomics. In: *Principles of Pharmacoeconomics*, Second Edition, edited by J. L. Bootman, R. J. Townsend, and W. F. McGhan. Cincinnati, OH: Harvey Whitney Book Company.

Nightingale, S. L. (1995). Challenges in international harmonization. *Drug Information Journal* 29:1-9.

U.S. Office of Technology Assessment. (1993). *Pharmaceutical R&D: Costs, Risks and Rewards.* Publication OTA-H-552. Washington, DC: U.S. Congress.

Wechsler, J. (1991). The high cost of prescription drugs. *Pharmaceutical Executive* 11:12-17.

Wyse R., S. Peel, and S. Kirby. (1997). Health economics in early drug development. *Scrip Magazine* 63:40-43.

Chapter 4

Luce, B. R. and A. Elixhauser. (1996). Socioeconomic evaluation and the health care industry. In: *Studies in Pharmaceutical Economics*, edited by M. C. Smith. Binghamton, NY: Pharmaceutical Products Press, an imprint of The Haworth Press, Inc.

Smith, D. H., D. C. Malone, K. A. Lawson, L. J. Okamoto, C. Battista, and W. B. Saunders. (1997). A national estimate of the economic costs of asthma. *American Journal of Respiratory and Critical Care Medicine* 156(3, Part 1): 787-793.

Sonnenberg, A. and J. E. Everhart. (1997). Health impact of peptic ulcer in the United States. *American Journal of Gastroenterology* 92(4):614-620.

Swinburn, B., T. Ashton, J. Gillespie, B. Cox, A. Menon, D. Simmons, and J. Birkbeck. (1997). Health care costs of obesity in New Zealand. *International Journal of Obesity and Related Metabolic Disorders* 21(10):891-896.

Taylor, T. N. (1997). The medical economics of stroke. *Drugs* 54(Suppl 3):51-57.

Wilson, L. (1997). Cost-of-illness of scleroderma: The case for rare diseases. *Seminars in Arthritis and Rheumatology* 27(2):73-84.

Chapter 5

Asch, J. and J. F. Wedgwood. (1997). Optimizing the approach to anemia in the preterm infant: Is there a role for erythropoietin therapy? *Journal of Perinatology* 17(4):276-282.

Deltenre, M. and K. O. Ilunga. (1997). *Helicobacter pylori* eradication in duodenal ulcer disease is cost-beneficial: A Belgian model. *Journal of Physiology and Pharmacology* 48(Suppl 4):107-113.

Drummond, M. F., B. J. O'Brien, G. L. Stoddart, and G. Torrance. (1997). *Methods for the Economic Evaluation of Health Care Programmes*, Second Edition. See chapter "Cost-benefit analysis." Oxford: Oxford University Press.

Feldstein, P. J. (1993). *Health Care Economics*, Fourth Edition. See chapter "An introduction to the economics of medical care." Albany, NY: Delmar Publishers, Inc.

McGhan, W. F. (1996). Cost-benefit analysis. *Principles of Pharmacoeconomics*, Second Edition, edited by J. L. Bootman, R. J. Townsend, and W. F. McGhan. Cincinnati, OH: Harvey Whitney Books Company.

Scott, W. G. and H. M. Scott. (1996). Economic evaluation of vaccination against influenza in New Zealand. *PharmacoEconomics* 9(1):51-60.

Timpka, T., M. Leijon, G. Karlsson, L. Svensson, and P. Bjurulf. (1997). Long-term economic effects of team-based clinical case management of patients with chronic minor disease and long-term absence from working life. *Scandinavian Journal of Social Medicine* 25(4):229-237.

Woolf, A., J. Wieler, and D. Greenes. (1997). Costs of poison-related hospitalizations at an urban teaching hospital for children. *Archives of Pediatrics and Adolescent Medicine* 151(7):719-723.

Chapter 6

Adamcik, B. A. (1997). *Pharmacy and the U.S. Health Care System*, Second Edition, edited by J. E. Fincham and A. I. Wertheimer. See chapter "The consumers of health care." Binghamton, NY: Pharmaceutical Products Press, an imprint of The Haworth Press, Inc.

Chrischilles, E. A. (1996). Cost-effectiveness analysis. In: *Principles of Pharmacoeconomics*, Second Edition, edited by J. L. Bootman, R. J. Townsend, and W. F. McGhan. Cincinnati, OH: Harvey Whitney Books Company.

Drummond, M. F., B. J. O'Brien, G. L. Stoddart, and G. Torrance. (1997). *Methods for the Economic Evaluation of Health Care Programmes*. See chapter "Cost-effectiveness analysis." Oxford: Oxford University Press.

Eisenstein, E. L., E. D. Peterson, J. G. Jollis, B. E. Tardiff, R. M. Califf, J. D. Knight, and D. B. Mark. (1997). Assessing the value of newer pharmacologic agents in non-ST elevation patients: A decision support system application. *Proceedings of the AMIA Annual Fall Symposium*, 273-277.

Freeman, R. A. (1996). Health policy initiatives and the utility of economic research. In: *Studies in Pharmaceutical Economics,* edited by M. C. Smith. Binghamton, NY: Pharmaceutical Products Press, an imprint of The Haworth Press, Inc.

Macdonald, J. S. (1997). Adjuvant therapy for colon cancer. *CA: A Cancer Journal for Clinicians* 47(4):243-256.

McMurray, J. J., A. McGuire, A. P. Davie, and D. Hughes. (1997). Cost-effectiveness of different ACE inhibitor treatment scenarios post-myocardial infarction. *European Heart Journal* 18(9):1411-1415.

Perreault, S., V. H. Hamilton, F. Lavoie, and S. Grover. (1998). Treating hyperlipidemia for the primary prevention of coronary disease. Are higher dosages of lovastatin cost-effective? *Archives of Internal Medicine* 158(4):375-381.

Roos, B. R., M. R. van Cleeff, W. A. Githui, L. Kivihya-Ndugga, J. A. Odhiambo, D. K. Kibuga, and P. R. Klatser. (1998). Cost-effectiveness of the polymerase chain reaction versus smear examination for the diagnosis of tuberculosis in Kenya: A theoretical model. *International Journal of Tuberculosis and Lung Disease* 2(3):235-241.

Chapter 7

Cassileth, B. R. (1992). Principles of quality of life assessment in cancer chemotherapy. *PharmacoEconomics* 2(4):279-284.

Coons, S. J. and R. M. Kaplan. (1996). Cost-utility analysis. In: *Principles of Pharmacoeconomics,* Second Edition, edited by J. L. Bootman, R. J. Townsend, and W. F. McGhan. Cincinnati, OH: Harvey Whitney Books Company.

Drummond, M. F., B. J. O'Brien, G. L. Stoddart, and G. Torrance. (1997). *Methods for the Economic Evaluation of Health Care Programmes,* Second Edition. See chapter "Cost-utility analysis." Oxford: Oxford University Press.

Gartner, S. H., M. A. Sevick, R. J. Keenan, and G. J. Chen. (1997). Cost-utility of lung transplantation: A pilot study. *Journal of Heart and Lung Transplantation* 16(11):1129-1134.

Holtgrave, D. R., and S. D. Pinkerton. (1997). Updates of cost of illness and quality of life estimates for use in economic evaluations of HIV prevention programs. *Journal of Acquired Immune Deficiency Syndromes and Human Retrovirology* 16(1):54-62.

Konski, A., P. Bracy, S. Weiss, and P. Grigsby. (1997). Cost-utility analysis of a malignant glioma protocol. *International Journal of Radiation Oncology, Biology, Physics* 39(3): 575-578.

Moore, R. D. and R. E. Chaisson. (1997). Cost-utility analysis of prophylactic treatment with oral ganciclovir for cytomegalovirus retinitis. *Journal of Acquired Immune Deficiency Syndromes and Human Retrovirology* 16(1):15-21.

Nord, E. (1994). The QALY—a measure of social value rather than individual utility? *Health Economics* 3:89-93.

Pathak, D. S. (1996). QALYs in health outcomes research: Representation of real preferences or another numerical abstraction? In: *Studies in Pharmaceutical Economics,* edited by M. C. Smith. Binghamton, NY: Pharmaceutical Products Press, an imprint of The Haworth Press, Inc.

Souetre, E. J., W. Qing, and M. Hardens. (1994). Methodological approaches to pharmaco-economics. *Fundamental and Clinical Pharmacology* 8:101-107.

Yee, G. C. (1997). Cost-utility analysis of taxane therapy. *American Journal of Health Systems and Pharmacy* 54(24, Suppl 2):S11-S15.

Chapter 8

Atkinson, K., S. Tokmakajian, W. Watson, and J. Gregor. (1997). Evaluation of the endomysial antibody for celiac disease: Operating properties and associated cost implications in clinical practice. *Canadian Journal of Gastroenterolo gy* 11(8): 673-677.

Birnie, E., W. M. Monincx, H. A. Zondervan, P. M. Bossuyt, and G. J. Bonsel. (1997). Cost-minimization analysis of domiciliary antenatal fetal monitoring in high risk pregnancies. *Obstetrics and Gynecology* 89(6):925-929.

Bootman, J. L., R. J. Townsend, and W. F. McGhan. (1996). Introduction to pharmacoeconomics. In: *Principles of Pharmacoeconomics,* Second Edition, edited by J. L. Bootman, R. J. Townsend, and W. F. McGhan. Cincinnati, OH: Harvey Whitney Books Company.

Drummond, M. F., B. J. O'Brien, G. L. Stoddart, and G. Torrance. (1997). *Methods for the Economic Evaluation of Health Care Programmes.* See chapter "Basic types of economic evaluation." Oxford: Oxford University Press.

Hilleman, D. E., B. D. Lucas Jr., S. M. Mohiuddin, and M. J. Holmberg. (1997). Cost-minimization analysis of intravenous adenosine and dipyridamole in thallous chloride TI 201 SPECT myocardial perfusion imaging. *Annals of Pharmacotherapy* 31(9):974-979.

Melton, S. T., C. K. Kirkwood, T. W. Farrar, D. D. Brink, and N. V. Carroll. (1997). Economic evaluation of paroxetine and imipramine in depressed outpatients. *Psychopharmacology Bulletin* 33(1):93-100.

Messick, C. R., M. Mamdani, I. R. McNicholl, L. H. Danziger, K. A. Rodvold, R. E. Condon, A. P. Walker, and C. E. Edmiston Jr. (1998). Pharmacoeconomic analysis of ampicillin-sulbactam versus cefoxitin in the treatment of intra-abdominal infections. *Pharmacotherapy* 18(1):175-183

Chapter 9

Abbott, E. A. (1884). Flatland: A Romance of Many Dimensions. London: Seeley & Company (original publication).

Asch, D. A. and J. C. Hershey. (1995). Why some health policies don't make sense at the bedside. *Annals of Internal Medicine* 122(11):846-850.

Davidoff, A. J. and N. R. Powe. (1996). The role of perspective in defining economic measures for the evaluation of medical technology. *International Journal of Technology Assessment in Health Care* 12(1):9-21.

Szucs, T. D. and L. G. Mantovani. (1997). The perspective of a pharmacoeconomic study: Targeting for audiences. *Pharmacological Research* 35(5):471-475.

Chapter 10

Boyer, J. G., R. J. Townsend, P. E. Stang, and H. M. Arrighi. (1998). Quality of life: Outcome assessment in pharmacoepidemiologic studies. In: *Pharmacoepidemiology: An Introduction*, Third Edition, edited by A. G. Hartzema, M. S. Porta, and H. H. Tilson. Cincinnati, OH: Harvey Whitney Books Company.

Drummond, M. F., B. J. O'Brien, G. L. Stoddart, and G. Torrance. (1997). *Methods for the Economic Evaluation of Health Care Programmes,* Second Edition. See chapter "Critical assessment of economic evaluation." Oxford: Oxford University Press.

Luce, B. R. and A. Elixhauser. (1996). Socioeconomic evaluation and the health care industry. In: *Studies in Pharmaceutical Economics,* edited by M. C. Smith. Binghamton, NY: Pharmaceutical Products Press, an imprint of The Haworth Press, Inc.

Testa, M. A., and J. F. Nackley. (1994). Methods for quality-of-life studies. *Annual Review of Public Health* 15:535-559.

Chapter 11

Drummond, M. F., B. J. O'Brien, G. L. Stoddart, and G. Torrance. (1997a). *Methods for the Economic Evaluation of Health Care Programmes*, Second Edition. See chapter "Cost analysis." Oxford: Oxford University Press.

Drummond, M. F., B. J. O'Brien, G. L. Stoddart, and G. Torrance. (1997b). *Methods for the Economic Evaluation of Health Care Programmes*, Second Edition. See chapter "Critical assessment of economic evaluation." Oxford: Oxford University Press.

Larson, L. N. (1996). Cost determination and analysis. In: *Principles of Pharmacoeconomics*, Second Edition, edited by J. L. Bootman, R. J. Townsend, and W. F. McGhan. Cincinnati, OH: Harvey Whitney Books Company.

Pindyck, R. S. and D. L. Rubinfeld. (1997). *Microeconomics*, Fourth Edition. See chapter "The cost of production." Upper Saddle River, NJ: Prentice-Hall, Inc., a Simon and Schuster Company.

Chapter 12

Briggs, A. and M. Sculpher. (1995). Sensitivity analysis in economic evaluation: A review of published studies. *Health Economics* 4:355-371.

Drummond, M. F., B. J. O'Brien, G. L. Stoddart, and G. Torrance. (1997). *Methods for the Economic Evaluation of Health Care Programmes*, Second Edition. See chapter "Cost-effectiveness analysis." Oxford: Oxford University Press.

Luce, B. R. and A. Elixhauser. (1996). Socioeconomic evaluation and the health care industry. In: *Studies in Pharmaceutical Economics*, edited by M. C. Smith. Binghamton, NY: Pharmaceutical Products Press, an imprint of The Haworth Press, Inc.

Chapter 13

Bonk, R. J. (1998). *Medical Writing in Drug Development: A Practical Guide for Pharmaceutical Research.* See chapter "Manuscripts in scientific journals." Binghamton, NY: Pharmaceutical Products Press, an imprint of The Haworth Press, Inc.

Drummond, M. F. and T. O. Jefferson, on behalf of the BMJ (*British Medical Journal*) Economic Evaluation Working Party. (1996). Guidelines for authors and peer reviewers of economic submissions to the BMJ. *British Medical Journal* 313(7052):275-283.

Jefferson, T. and V. Demicheli. (1995). Are guidelines for peer-reviewing economic evaluations necessary? A survey of current editorial practice. *Health Economics* 4:383-388.

Kassirer, J. P. and M. Angell. (1994). The *Journal's* policy on cost-effectiveness analyses. *New England Journal of Medicine* 331(10):669-670.

Task Force on Principles for Economic Analysis of Health Care Technology. (1995). Economic analysis of health care technology: A report on principles. *Annals of Internal Medicine* 123(1):61-70.

Chapter 14

Bloom, B. S. and A. M. Fendrick. (1996). Timing and timeliness in medical care evaluation. *PharmacoEconomics* 9(3):183-187.

Bonk, R. J. (1998). *Medical Writing in Drug Development: A Practical Guide for Pharmaceutical Research.* See chapter "Challenges of broadening audiences." Binghamton, NY: Pharmaceutical Products Press, an imprint of The Haworth Press, Inc.

Freemantle, N. and A. Maynard. (1994). Something rotten in the state of clinical and economic evaluations? *Health Economics* 3:63-67.

Henry, D. (1992). Economic analysis as an aid to subsidisation decisions. The development of Australian guidelines for pharmaceuticals. *PharmacoEconomics* 1(1):54-67.

Langley, P. C. (1993). The role of pharmacoeconomic guidelines for formulary approval: The Australian experience. *Clinical Therapeutics* 15(6):1154-1176.

Langley, P. C. (1996). The November 1995 revised Australian guidelines for the economic evaluation of pharmaceuticals. *PharmacoEconomics* 9(4):341-352.

Sanchez, L. A. (1996). Pharmacoeconomics and formulary decision making. *PharmacoEconomics* 9(Suppl 1):16-25.

Task Force on Principles for Economic Analysis of Health Care Technology. (1995). Economic analysis of health care technology: A report on principles. *Annals of Internal Medicine* 123(1):61-70.

Index

Page numbers followed by the letter "i" indicate illustrations; those followed by the letter "t" indicate tables.

Order Your Own Copy of
This Important Book for Your Personal Library!

PHARMACOECONOMICS IN PERSPECTIVE
A Primer on Research, Techniques, and Information

_____ in hardbound at $49.95 (ISBN: 0-7890-0561-1)

COST OF BOOKS_____

OUTSIDE USA/CANADA/
MEXICO: ADD 20%_____

POSTAGE & HANDLING_____
*(US: $3.00 for first book & $1.25
for each additional book)
Outside US: $4.75 for first book
& $1.75 for each additional book)*

SUBTOTAL_____

IN CANADA: ADD 7% GST_____

STATE TAX_____
*(NY, OH & MN residents, please
add appropriate local sales tax)*

FINAL TOTAL_____
*(If paying in Canadian funds,
convert using the current
exchange rate. UNESCO
coupons welcome.)*

☐ **BILL ME LATER:** ($5 service charge will be added)
(Bill-me option is good on US/Canada/Mexico orders only;
not good to jobbers, wholesalers, or subscription agencies.)

☐ Check here if billing address is different from
shipping address and attach purchase order and
billing address information.

Signature_____

☐ **PAYMENT ENCLOSED: $** _____

☐ **PLEASE CHARGE TO MY CREDIT CARD.**

☐ Visa ☐ MasterCard ☐ AmEx ☐ Discover
☐ Diner's Club

Account # _____

Exp. Date _____

Signature _____

Prices in US dollars and subject to change without notice.

NAME _____

INSTITUTION _____

ADDRESS _____

CITY _____

STATE/ZIP _____

COUNTRY _____ COUNTY (NY residents only) _____

TEL _____ FAX _____

E-MAIL_____
May we use your e-mail address for confirmations and other types of information? ☐ Yes ☐ No

Order From Your Local Bookstore or Directly From
The Haworth Press, Inc.
10 Alice Street, Binghamton, New York 13904-1580 • USA
TELEPHONE: 1-800-HAWORTH (1-800-429-6784) / Outside US/Canada: (607) 722-5857
FAX: 1-800-895-0582 / Outside US/Canada: (607) 772-6362
E-mail: getinfo@haworthpressinc.com
PLEASE PHOTOCOPY THIS FORM FOR YOUR PERSONAL USE.

BOF96

FORTHCOMING and RECENTLY PUBLISHED BOOKS
FROM HAWORTH PHARMACEUTICAL PRODUCTS PRESS

Take 20% Off Each Book! SPECIAL OFFER

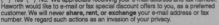